JEShorphree

10 Church Hill

E 17.

THE BEGINNINGS
OF
ENGLISH OVERSEAS ENTERPRISE
A PRELUDE TO THE EMPIRE

OXFORD UNIVERSITY PRESS

LONDON   EDINBURGH   GLASGOW   NEW YORK
TORONTO MELBOURNE CAPE TOWN BOMBAY

HUMPHREY MILFORD
PUBLISHER TO THE UNIVERSITY

THE BEGINNINGS OF
ENGLISH OVERSEAS
ENTERPRISE

A PRELUDE TO THE EMPIRE

BY

SIR C. P. LUCAS
K.C.B., K.C.M.G.

OXFORD
AT THE CLARENDON PRESS
1917

PREFACE

THIS book is intended to give an account, from standard sources, of the earliest English associations, in connexion with trade beyond the seas, principally of the Merchant Adventurers of England, whose importance seems to me to have been strangely minimized or ignored in most text-books of English or British history. Much of the book is concerned with times later than the Middle Ages, my object being to try to illustrate the continuity of English history and the cardinal fact that the British Empire is the result of growth. A large number of notes and references have been included, in the hope of saving some time and trouble to students, of what I have found to be a most difficult and laborious subject. I am indebted to Miss K. M. Eliot for help in connexion with Henry the Fourth's Charter.

C. P. LUCAS.

March, 1917.

CONTENTS

CHAPTER I

PRELIMINARY

AT all times Britain must have had some overseas trade, some dealings with the mainland which lies so near its shores. Coming and going of men implies interchange of commodities of one kind or another, traffic being scanty when there is anarchy on land and piracy at sea, plentiful when there is strong rule on land and vigilant guardianship of the water.

British tin appears to have been exploited and exported for some three centuries before the Christian era, finding its way across the Straits of Dover and through France to Marseilles. Under Roman rule tin, lead, and iron were worked and exported, lead, mentioned by both Caesar and Tacitus, being, it would seem, a special attraction.[1] Among other exports in Roman times, corn was sent over to Gaul and to the Rhine country, while British cloth is mentioned in an Edict of Diocletian.[2] London, according to Tacitus, was even at the beginning of the Roman occupation of the island, in A.D. 61,

Early British traffic.

---

[1] See Mommsen, *Provinces of the Roman Empire*, trans., 1886 ed., vol. i, p. 176.

[2] Haverfield, *The Romanization of Roman Britain*, 3rd ed., 1915, p. 77.

a great resort for merchants and trading vessels.[1]
Under the Anglo-Saxon and Danish kings trade
went on. The latter-day story of our Empire
teaches that the mission-field is also the resort of
the trader, and the introduction of Christianity into
England must have meant an increase of commercial as well as spiritual communication between
the island and Western Europe. English merchants
were busy on the Continent in the days of Charle-
magne,[2] and there was a complaint that at that
time the Anglo-Saxons exported garments of smaller
size than formerly.[3] While King Alfred's and
King Edgar's ships kept the Narrow Seas, traders
could cross and recross the Channel in safety ; and
under Edgar's minister, Dunstan, foreign merchants
multiplied in London. When the Danish king,
Canute, gave peace to England and joined her to
Scandinavia, the North Sea was, for the time being,
under one strong hand, and sea-borne traffic must
have been abundant. Honest trade there was in
these early centuries, and there was also a nefarious
slave traffic. According to the old story, it was
the spectacle of Anglo-Saxon boys for sale in the
slave-market at Rome that led to the mission of

---

[1] *Annals*, xiv. 33.

[2] See *The League between Carolus Magnus and Offa King of Mercia
concerning safe trade of the English merchants in all the Emperor's
dominion*, which Hakluyt quotes from William of Malmesbury (Hakluyt, Maclehose, 1903 ed., vol. i, pp. 310–11). The references given to
Hakluyt in succeeding notes are all from this edition.

[3] Lappenberg, *England under the Anglo-Saxon Kings* (Thorpe's
translation, 1845, vol. ii, p. 364).

Augustine, and Bristol was notorious for shipping
slaves to Ireland.

But the Norman Conquest gave to the overseas Effect of
trade of England life and substance beyond all Norman
that had gone before.   At a time when the whole Conquest.
Western world was beginning to move from dark-
ness to light, it linked the island politically and
commercially to the lands to which it is geographically adjacent, and swept the islanders into currents,
like the Crusades, which carried men and ships to
distant seas.   On Southern Britain the conquerors
imposed in ruthless fashion the conditions necessary
for trade : comparative peace, union, and continuity
of rule.   A line of foreign kings brought over the
Channel a following of foreign merchants and workmen, minded to develop the resources of England
in connexion with and in reference to their old
homes.   What their old homes in France and
Flanders were most glad to take, and what England
could most readily provide, was wool.   In the English
eleventh century, before the Conquest, the Flemish cloth.
towns had become notable centres of cloth-making,
and wool had become a great article of export from
England to those towns.   After the Conquest the
export grew, and for centuries wool and cloth
represented the main trading wealth of England.

In the reign of James I, when the English were
at length beginning to take root beyond the ocean,
wool and cloth were still pre-eminent among English
exports.   Lord Justice Coke enumerated the five

staple merchandises of England, wool, woolfels,
leather, lead, and tin ; and wool and cloth he rated
as 'the worthiest and richest commodity of this
kingdom ; for divide our native commodities exported into ten parts, and that which comes from
the sheep's back is nine parts in value of the ten,
and setteth great numbers of people on work'.[1]
A pamphlet of the year 1645, attacking the monopoly
of the British cloth trade, which had been acquired
by the Merchant Adventurers, speaks of 'wool and
the draping and merchandising thereof' as 'the
Cape commodity, wherewith nature, the handmaid
of God Almighty, hath furnished this island';[2]
and in a later pamphlet of 1681 the woollen trade
of England is said to be 'like the water to the
mill that driveth round the wheel of all other
trades'.[3]

In the course of nature a young country, when it
begins to export, exports raw produce, importing in
exchange manufactured articles. As the country
becomes mature, as population grows and civilization spreads within its borders, manufactures and
industries come into being and multiply, more and

[1] Coke on Littleton, 1809 ed., vol. iv, p. 41 note.
[2] *A discourse consisting of motives for the enlargement and freedom of
trade, especially that of cloth and other woollen manufactures, engrossed
at present contrary to the law of nature, the law of nations, and the laws
of this kingdom, by a company of private men who style themselves Merchant Adventurers*, 1645, p. 5. (British Museum Tracts on Wool,
712. g. $\frac{16}{2}$.)
[3] *The Trade of England revived and the abuses thereof rectified, &c.*,
1681, p. 2. (B. M. 712. g. $\frac{16}{26}$.)

more of the raw produce is used at home, and the export of manufactured articles takes in an increasing degree the place of the export of raw produce. Thus it was that in the early Middle Ages the main English export was wool, while at a later date the main export was cloth, and the development of the cloth industry is commonly taken to have dated from the reign of Edward III, the king who imported Flemish clothmakers to teach the English the secrets of their art. But it must not be supposed that one age for England was wholly an age of wool and another age wholly an age of cloth, or that the first of the early English Mercantile Associations for overseas trade, the Merchants of the Staple, dealt only in wool, and the later company, the Merchant Adventurers, dealt only in cloth.[1] From time im- Antiquity memorial there was clothmaking of one kind and of British cloth. another in Britain, as shown by the mention of British cloth in Diocletian's time; and, long before Edward III laid the foundation of the cloth industry

---

[1] Thus Gerard Malynes, the great champion of the Staplers, in the early part of the seventeenth century, in *The Maintenance of Free Trade*, &c., 1622, p. 50, writes, 'The Merchants of the Staple, from all the Staple ports, as London, Westminster, Bristol, Southampton, Hull, Boystone (? Boston) and Newcastle have hitherto exported either cloth or wool or both, which now they may not'; and in *The Center of the Circle of Commerce*, 1623, pp. 86–7, he maintains that the Staplers exported cloth before the Merchant Adventurers had ever come into being. It must always be borne in mind that the Staplers dealt with all staple articles of merchandise; wool was their speciality, but only because wool was by far the most important of these articles. Whether cloth was a staple article was a moot point. (See below, pp. 53–5.)

as a standard industry for Englishmen, some English cloths were in demand in foreign markets. It is stated that there were woollen manufactures in England in the reigns of Henry II and Richard I, which died out in the two succeeding reigns, to be revived later by Edward III. It is certain that the weavers were the oldest or one of the oldest of the London guilds ; that the London weavers were given some kind of charter by the first Henry, another by the second ; that there were ancient laws or by-laws in various English cities, regulating the weavers' craft ; that Richard I issued an assize of cloth ; and that an article of Magna Charta fixed what the breadth of dyed cloth should be.[1] Nor was foreign tuition in clothmaking wanting before Edward III became king. The Norman Conquest was not merely a conquest : it was a colonization. Matilda of Flanders was the Conqueror's consort ; and, with a Flemish lady on the throne of England, there were strong inducements for Flemish craftsmen to cross the channel. In the reign of Henry I more Flemings came in, flooded out from their own country, and these immigrants may well have been responsible for an earlier stage in skilled clothmaking in England, as the Flemings, whom

---

[1] Magna Charta, cap. xxv : 'and one breadth of dyed cloth, russets and haberjects, that is to say, two yards within the lists' (Coke on Littleton, 1809 ed., vol. iv, p. 41). The note says, 'True it is that broad cloths were made, though in small number, at the time, and long before this statute, but in the beginning of the reign of Edward III the same came to so great perfection, &c.'

Edward III brought over, were responsible for its new birth.[1]

But, without impugning the antiquity of the English cloth industry, it is beyond question that in the early Middle Ages England was to France and Flanders what Australia is to England and Europe at the present day, pre-eminently a wool producing and exporting country, and that with this raw product of wool the Merchants of the Staple were mainly concerned. They were the eldest of three great mediaeval companies, or rather groups of merchants, the other two being the Merchant Adventurers and the Eastland merchants. Of the three the Merchant Adventurers were incomparably the greatest and the most interesting historically ; but all the three deserve attention : they contained within them the seeds of the coming time.

It would be difficult to find any subject in English history more obscure, more full of disputable points, than that of these early companies. When did they begin ? When did they end ? In what sense were they companies at all ? Where were their head-

The three great mediaeval companies.

---

[1] For the substance of this paragraph see Anderson, *An Historical and Geographical deduction of the Origin of Commerce from the earliest accounts to the present time* (1764) ; Macpherson, *Annals of Commerce,* 1805 ; Cunningham, *Growth of English Industry and Commerce*, vol. i, Early and Middle Ages, 5th ed., 1910; Salzmann, *English Industries of the Middle Ages*, 1913, &c. Archdeacon Cunningham, p. 647, says that weavers are not mentioned in Domesday, but Lappenberg would read the panifici (bakers), who are mentioned in Domesday at Stamford, pannifici (clothmakers), *ut sup.*, vol. ii, p. 363.

quarters? Whom did they include and whom did
they exclude? What were their special spheres of
activity? The dates are uncertain: the facts are
doubtful: the authorities differ: it is only possible
to attempt to piece together some general outline.

Slow evo-
lution of
English
overseas
trade.

They represent the first efforts in English history
at mercantile co-operation in respect of overseas
trade. In the beginning of trading enterprise, in
the early Middle Ages, all was tentative and rudi-
mentary. It is idle to look for and hope to light
upon well-defined landmarks, well-ascertained birth-
days, on which, as in later times, this or that
historic company came into the world under the
provisions of unmistakable charters with unmistakable objects. The process was one of slow
evolution. There were traders in England, some
aliens, some native born; the proportion of the
aliens to the native born was largest in the earliest
stages; and in the earliest stages the alien merchants in the main handled the export trade,[1] for they
were traders who had come into a more or less
barbarous and undeveloped island from lands slightly
more advanced in civilization. As time went on,
what had been indefinite gradually took form and

---

[1] 'Until the end of the thirteenth century, the greater part of the
export trade from England was in foreign hands' (*The Place of the
reign of Edward II in English History*, by Professor Tout, 1914, p. 242).
Cf. Anderson (*ut sup.*, vol. i, p. 117), 'What the statutes and ordinances
of early times called notable merchants, were only those of the Staple,
who at first were all foreigners, as appears by Magna Charta, as well
as by the Statute of the Staple 27th of Edward III ann. 1353, which
prohibits English merchants from carrying staple commodities.'

shape. Particular products and industries emerged ;
and out of the commonalty of merchants some of the
traders formed one kind of connexion and others
another ; some dealt with one kind of produce,
others with another. In time the line between
aliens and native born began to be more clearly
drawn, and the native born began to take into their
own hands a larger proportion of the trade. In
time the need grew up for recognized depôts and
markets, at first for trade as a whole, later for particular kinds of trade ; trade centres in England
were required, and trade centres in the lands to
which English produce was sent ; and rules and
regulations in connexion with the trade centres
were seen to be for the obvious convenience of the
traders and for the obvious advantage of the governments and their revenues. In time English merchants gained a footing in foreign lands and established themselves at the trade centres : they grouped
themselves together at one centre or another, regulated their group among themselves, or tried to do
so, and then proceeded to have their governor and
their regulations recognized by their king at home.
This seems to have formed the earliest kind of
charter for such bodies as the Merchant Adventurers
and the Eastlanders, kings and merchants alike
discerning in a growing degree the use of and the
necessity for fixed markets, accredited traders, and
regulated traffic.

As the companies grew older and stronger, as

what had been without form and void took substance and shape and clearly defined outline : as nations, governments, merchants, products, all gradually crystallized, successively revised versions of the charters showed more clearness and increasing definition. The merchants covered by one charter became more and more distinct from the merchants covered by another; the provisions for law and order, which had been the sole object of the old charters—because, when the old charters were granted, public law and order was in the most elementary stage—gave way to provisions for safeguarding and intensifying a trade monopoly; in other words, charters in a more modern sense came into being. But in the beginning it was not so, and it is futile to try to read into the past what was not and could not be in existence.

Furthermore, it must be borne in mind that after the general body, the commonalty of merchants, had become subdivided into distinct bodies, Staplers, Merchant Adventurers, Eastlanders, and the like, while the companies were wholly distinct from one another, on the other hand then, as now, many members of one company were also members of another : many, if not most, of the Staplers were Merchant Adventurers also, and the Merchant Adventurers and Eastlanders were largely composed of the same personnel.

The old companies

So far as these old companies can be classed as companies in the ordinary sense of the term, they were regulated not joint-stock companies. They ^{were} were enlarged editions of the city or trade guild, in ^{regulated com-} that their members who, at any rate in the case of ^{panies.} the Merchant Adventurers, became members as a rule by payment of a fee or Hanse, as it was styled in old days, enjoyed the safeguards to their trade which their corporation provided, but traded on their own account. 'The Company of Merchants Adventurers', wrote their Secretary Wheeler at the beginning of the seventeenth century, 'hath no bank, nor common stock, nor common factor to buy or sell for the whole company, but every man tradeth apart, and particularly with his own stock, and with his own factor or servant.'[1] So it had been from the beginning: it was a case of evolution again: the guild, which had proved so effective for municipal trading, was expanded to meet the purposes of overseas trade. Wheeler wrote immediately after the coming to birth of the East India Company, and in the story of the East India Company the development of joint-stock companies out of regulated companies can be clearly traced, the subscriptions by East India merchants to particular voyages, in the early days of the company, marking the stage of transition from regulation to joint-stock.[2]

[1] *A Treatise of Commerce, &c.*, by John Wheeler, secretary to the Merchants Adventurers, 1601, p. 143.

[2] The Muscovy Company, however, was from the first a joint-stock company, and the Levant Company started as a joint-stock company, becoming afterwards a regulated company.

CHAPTER II

THE MERCHANTS OF THE STAPLE

The Merchants of the Staple : not a company in the ordinary sense.

THE Merchants of the Staple hardly come under the category even of a regulated company. In their later days, in the reigns of Queen Elizabeth and James I, they figure as a regulated company, 'The Mayor Constables and Fellowship of the Merchants of the Staple of England'; but by this time the Staple in its old sense was obsolete. It was not so much a case of a company as of a system, the staple system being a Government organization, the machinery of which was provided by the merchants concerned with the trade.

A great authority tells us that 'the system of the staple was, it would seem, a combination of the principle of the guild and of the royal privilege of establishing fairs and markets'.[1] Through all the different shades of meaning of the word staple, so the etymologists say, there runs one and the same sense of firmness or fixity.[2] Something firm, some-

[1] Stubbs, *Constitutional History of England*, 1880 ed., vol. ii, pp. 447–8.
[2] See Skeat, *Etymological Dictionary*, s.v. The *New English Dictionary* says that the general sense at the root of the word is that of 'something supporting'; it also says that the English word (in this trade sense) is not found earlier than 1423, though 'estaple' and 'stapula' are found from Edward II's reign onwards.

thing assured, some fixed point, a thing, a place, a rule, a standard, was the one thing needful amid troubled, insecure, dangerous conditions, such as prevailed in the changing early youth of England. Wool grew to be a leading English product : it came to stay : it became a staple article of merchandise. As such, it was all-important for revenue purposes, and needy kings were at pains to assure the subsidies which could be derived from this source. The merchants who dealt in wool The staple wished, for their part, to safeguard the trade and to system. maintain the standard of the wool.[1] Kings and subjects, in short, combined to staple the industry, to standardize it, to regulate it, to make it firm. Hence arose the system of establishing particular centres, at which alone the buying and selling for export should be conducted, and the word staple was used more especially to designate these central marts or markets.[2]

The system was intelligible and had its merits ; but its value must have been largely nullified by

[1] See what is said in the Introduction to *The Cely Papers, Selections from the Correspondence and Memoranda of the Cely family, Merchants of the Staple, A.D. 1475–1488.* Edited for the Royal Historical Society by Henry Elliot Malden, 1900, Introduction, pp. x, xi.

[2] Thus Coke says, 'The word staple, anciently written estaple, cometh of the French word estape, which signifieth a mart or market' (Coke upon Littleton, 1809 ed., vol. vii, p. 238) ; and in Strype's enlargement of Stow's *Survey of London* it is stated that ' the word means the place where the market of such or such merchandise was kept, as herein in Westminster was the Woolstaple ' (Stow's *Survey*, 1720 ed., Bk. VI, p. 6).

the perpetual changes which took place. The markets were changed : the rules were changed : exceptions were made when it suited the kings' pockets. The merchants can never have known the kings' minds from one year to another, and the kings do not appear to have known their own. The constant vicissitudes which accompanied the staple system form a strange comment upon the fixity which the system was intended to provide, and which the term staple implies.

The Company of the Staple was a Melchizedek among companies. No one knows when it began or when it ended, if it has ended, for as late as 1887 its ghost had not been finally laid to rest.[1] There is a general consensus of opinion that it was the oldest of the mediaeval companies other than the guilds.

'It seemeth', wrote Stow in his *Survey of London* in the year 1603, 'that the marchants of this Staple be the most ancient marchants of this realm.'[2] Their

---

[1] See Carr, *Select Charters of Trading Companies, A.D. 1530–1707*, Selden Society, 1913, Introduction, p. xxi note ; and Gross, *The Gild Merchant*, 1890, vol. i, p. 145, and note.

[2] *A Survey of London*, by John Stow, reprinted from the text of 1603, with introduction and notes by Charles Lethbridge Kingsford, 1908, vol. ii, p. 104. Strype in his edition of Stow (1720) repeats this statement of Stow's in vol. ii, Bk. VI, p. 7; but in vol. ii, Bk. V, p. 259, he gives—which is not in the original Stow—a notice of the Merchants of the Staple as 'the first and most ancient English company of merchants, trading in wools', adding that they were incorporated by King Edward III, and on the same page a notice of the Merchant Adventurers as 'the ancientest company of merchants in England', incorporated in 1296 by King Edward I. Following Strype, Maitland, in his history of London, 1756, vol. ii, p. 1256, says that the Merchant Adventurers were incorporated by Edward I in

antiquity was emphasized in later times as against Antiquity of the Company of the Staple.
the Merchant Adventurers who supplanted them,
and who also claimed an ancient parentage. There
is a statement attributing the birth of the Staplers to
the year 1248. 'Some authors date the rise of the
first commercial society of English merchants, styled
of St. Thomas Becket, from this year, when they
are said to have had privileges granted them in the
Netherlands by John Duke of Brabant, whither it
seems they had begun to resort with our English
wool, lead, and tin, and to trade for their fine
woollen cloths, etc. From which society did the
company spring, styled the Merchants of the Staple
of England.'[1] The date 1267 is also given in the
same book, both dates being within the reign of
Henry III. It was the Merchant Adventurers who
more especially fathered themselves on Becket; but,
on the other hand, we are told that in the twenty-
fifth year of the reign of Edward III, i.e. in 1351–2,
that king 'appointed the Staple of wool to be kept
only at Canterbury, for the honour of St. Thomas'.[2]

1296, that this was 'the first incorporation of merchants erected in
this kingdom', and that 'the second company of merchants incorporated in England were those of the Staple', who were incorporated
by Edward III. All other authorities seem to give priority to the
merchants of the Staple.

[1] Anderson, *An Historical and Chronological deduction of the Origin
of Commerce*, 1764, vol. i, p. 117, and see p. 125.

[2] Stow (Kingsford), vol. ii, p. 103. In the charter given by
Edward IV in 1462 to the English merchants in the Netherlands to
elect a governor, which will be found in Hakluyt (Maclehose ed.,
vol. ii, pp. 147–58), one fourth of the fines was to be applied to 'the
repairing and maintenance of two chapels founded to the honour of

It can well be believed that either company found it convenient in later times to connect themselves with a saint made in England, so as to hallow their origin, to give it a national flavour, and by implication to date it back to the reign of Henry II ; while the fact that both Staplers and Merchant Adventurers claimed to be a Becket brotherhood indicates that in the beginnings of the wool trade Staplers and Merchant Adventurers were one, that neither Staplers nor Merchant Adventurers had as yet a separate existence.

All modern writers on the subject again agree that it was in the middle or the latter half of the thirteenth century, in the reign of Henry III or Edward I, that the staple system in some sort began, and that the first staple market was not in England but in Brabant or Flanders, at Antwerp or at Bruges. On the other hand, it is to be noted that Stow writes of a woolstaple being at Westminster at least as early as the reign of Edward I.[1]

St. Thomas of Canterbury by our said subjects, in the towns of Bruges in Flanders and of Middleborough in Zeland '.   Canterbury again was one of the staple towns named in the great statute of 1353.   The Mercers had special connexion with the Becket tradition.   Stow speaks of 'the Mercers chapel, sometime a hospital entitled of St. Thomas of Acon, or Acars ', founded by the sister of Thomas Becket and her husband.   (See Kingsford, i. 269.)

[1] Stow (Kingsford), vol. ii, p. 102, 'Touching this Woolstable, I read that in the reign of E—— the first, the staple being at Westminster, the parishioners of St. Margaret and marchants of the staple builded of new the said church, &c.'   Mrs. J. R. Green dates the beginning of the staple system from the first half of the thirteenth century (*Town Life in the Fifteenth Century*, 1894, vol. i, p. 45).   Professor Ashley says

There was, no doubt, in the ordinary English fashion, a slow and gradual growth of a system, as the trade slowly grew, private effort going on in front, and Government action following in its train. From the reign of Henry III, a staple or central market for English wool had come into being in the Low Countries, established not by any enactment but by convenience of the trade. In Edward I's reign, in The reign of Edward I. the year 1296, the Duke of Brabant gave a special charter of privileges to English merchants, which was renewed in 1305, and in 1297 he granted the port of Antwerp in fee to his father-in-law, the

that about the middle of the thirteenth century English merchants began exporting English products, and the staple came into existence, due to royal policy and initiative ; that the staple was usually in Flanders, and then almost always at Bruges, but also from time to time in Brabant at Antwerp (*An Introduction to English Economic History and Theory*. Part I, The Middle Ages, 2nd ed., 1892, pp. 111–12). Archdeacon Cunningham says that the Merchants of the Staple claimed to date as a separate body from the reign of Henry III, that Edward I 'named certain ports and forced the wool trade into particular channels so that the collection of the customs might be facilitated' (*ut sup.*, p. 311). Gross (*ut sup.*, vol. i, p. 140) states, 'The merchants of the staple used to claim that their privileges dated from the time of Henry III, but existing records do not refer to the staple before the time of Edward I. Previous to this reign the export trade was mainly in the hands of the German Hanse merchants.' Stubbs says that the growth of the system dates from Edward I, who bought Antwerp from the Duke of Brabant, and established there a foreign centre for the wool trade (*ut sup.*, vol. ii, pp. 447–8). Mr. Malden in his Introduction to *The Cely Papers* (*ut sup.*, p. viii) dates the system from Edward I. The last word on the subject seems to have been said by Professor Tout in *The Place of the reign of Edward II in English History*, pp. 241–66 : *The Establishment of the Compulsory Staple*. This admirable and exhaustive account has been mainly followed in the text.

English king, to be an entrepôt for English wool : at Antwerp the English merchants formed a more or less organized body, presided over by a mayor. In that same year, 1297, Edward I passed an ordinance for customs purposes, confining the export of wool and leather from England to certain specified English ports. Thus in his reign the export of wool from England was to some extent regulated by Government, while beyond the sea the English merchants, with their king's support, formed for themselves a staple market and some kind of corporation in connexion with the market.

The reign of Edward II. The ordinance of 1313.

A further stage was reached in the reign of Edward II. On the 20th of May 1313 the king and his council passed an ordinance providing that, inasmuch as both king and merchants had suffered from promiscuous selling of English wool in Brabant, Artois, and Flanders, the wool should be taken ' to a fixed staple to be ordained and assigned within any of the same lands by the mayor and community of the said merchants of our realm '. The mayor and council of the merchants were authorized to impose fines for contravention of the ordinance, which in England were to be enforced by the officers of the Government, while, if the goods of the offending merchants should be at a staple outside the royal jurisdiction, the mayor and council were left to exact reasonable punishment on their own authority, ' as they have hitherto been wont to do '. These last words are a clear indication that before this date the merchants had worked on staple lines, but now, for the first time, the custom of the traders was enforced by the authority of the Government.[1]

A sequel to the ordinance is given in Hakluyt under date the 18th of June 1320, and it is in the form of Instructions to the Collectors of Customs at the Port of London and other of the chief English ports of the time, calling attention to evasion of the ordinance of 1313.   This document is headed ' An ordinance of the Staple to bee holden at one certaine place '.[2]

The staple market for English wool was a valuable asset which princes and cities on the continent coveted.   In May 1314 Philip, King of France, applied to the King of England to compel English

[1] See *English Economic History, Select Documents* (Bland, Brown, and Tawney, 1914, pp. 178–80 and note), and see *The Place of the reign of Edward II in English History*, by Professor Tout (*ut sup.*, pp. 247–9). Professor Tout speaks of the ordinance of 1313 as 'the first known ordinance of the staple'. 'It put an end to the merely preferential staple, and set up a monopolistic staple in its place.' Macpherson, in his *Annals of Commerce* (i. 478–9), takes this year, 1313, as the date of the first definite origin of the Company of the Staple : he says ' they constituted such a society at Antwerp as the merchants of the Gildhall (i.e. the Hanse Merchants) did in London '. His account in these pages shows that he well understood the beginnings of the system.   The evidence for the statement that the Duke of Brabant granted Antwerp in fee to the King of England is an inspeximus of 21 March 1313 in Edward II's reign, which proves that the grant at this date still held good (Pat. 6 Edw. II, p. 2, m. 16, Rymer Record Ed., vol. ii, pt. I, p. 206).

[2] Hakluyt (*ut sup.*), vol. i, pp. 350–5.   Professor Tout (pp. 248–9 and note) mentions similar Instructions to the Collectors of Customs on 22 August 1313, in which the ports named are not in all cases the same as those given in Hakluyt.

merchants to bring their wool to a staple at St. Omer
in Artois, noting that they had previously had
a staple at Antwerp.[1] In December 1315 there
was a Government notification in England that
a conference would be called to consider the King
of France's wish for a staple between Calais and
the Seine.[2] In November 1318 summonses were
issued to English citizens and merchants to a conference to be held in London to discuss the establishment of a wool staple in Flanders, special mention
being made of John Charlton, ' mayor of the merchants of the said kingdom '.[3] As a matter of fact,
for nine or ten years from 1314 onwards the staple,
or at any rate the chief staple, was at St. Omer ;
it then gravitated for a short time to Bruges.

So far the staple, whether unofficial or official,
had always been on the Continent, but feeling was
gathering strength in England in favour of planting
it within the realm. In 1319 the king called a
conference of merchants, who, or some of whom,
advised him to establish two places in England for
the sale and purchase of wool, one on either side of
the river Trent, ' and that the law and usages and
franchises, which merchants repairing to the staple
in these times have had and used, they should use

[1] See Rymer under date 28 May 1314 (die martis post Penthe-
coston), and see Burgon's *Life and Times of Sir Thomas Gresham*,
1839, vol. i, p. 72 note. For a detailed narrative of the changes
of the staple at this period see Tout, *ut sup.*, pp. 250, &c.

[2] Rymer, 16 December 1315.

[3] Rymer, 22 November 1318.

and enjoy henceforth at the places where they shall be'. This is the first recorded proposal for having staple towns in England.[1] Seven years later, in May 1326, still in Edward II's reign, an ordinance was made, providing 'that the staple of the merchants and the merchandise of England, Ireland, and Wales, namely of wools, hides, woolfels, and tin, be holden in the same lands and nowhere else, and that too in the places below written'. Then follow eight towns for England, three for Ireland, three for Wales, and three tin staple towns in Cornwall and Devonshire. At these centres alien merchants were to buy their wool, hides, and tin, with liberty, after they had paid their dues, to carry their purchases into any friendly country; while the merchants of England, Ireland, and Wales, who desired to export, were to deposit their wool, hides, and tin at the staples for sale for fifteen days, after which time they might export at will. The staple towns, in short, were to be the only marts for export: here alone alien merchants might buy, and here alone native merchants might sell to aliens. All merchants, native or alien, were to be subject at the staples to the law merchant, and the wool merchants were to be given a Mayor of the Staples. Clothmaking was encouraged by prohibiting, in the case of the common people, the use of foreign cloth,

The ordinance of 1326.

---

[1] *English Economic History, Select Documents, ut sup.*, pp. 180–1, and see the *English Historical Review* of January, 1914, to which reference is made in the note.

and by the promise of privileges to weavers and dyers.[1]

This ordinance of 1326 clearly distinguishes between alien merchants and native born, between merchant strangers and the subjects of the king. In 1313 no such distinction was made : the same provisions were applied to all merchants, 'denizen and alien alike'. The ordinance evidently contemplated that the actual exporting should be mainly done by aliens, while the home market should be exclusively left to the native born ; and, as will be seen, a quarter of a century later the statute of 1353 actually made it a felony for a native dealer to export wool. Thus by the end of the reign of Edward II all the elements of the staple system, as it was developed in 1353, had come into being, a compulsory fixed market, the domiciling of the market within the realm, and discrimination between alien and native merchants ; the growing power of the native merchants being shown by bringing the market back into England, by limiting or beginning to limit the sphere of the alien merchants, and by placing them, together with the English merchants, under the control of a mayor.

The reign of Edward III.

Edward III began his reign with an enactment of

[1] *English Economic History*, pp. 181–4. The eight staple towns in England were Newcastle-upon-Tyne, York, Lincoln, Norwich, London, Winchester, Exeter, and Bristol. All these towns appear in the statute of 1353, Westminster being substituted for London, and London kept as the port of Westminster. Canterbury and Chichester were added to the list. (See below, p. 33.)

30 April 1327, forbidding English merchants to leave the kingdom until they belonged to a staple ;[1] but in the following year, 1328, he entirely reversed his father's policy, a statute being passed which provided ' that the staples beyond the sea and on'this side, ordained by Kings in times past, and the pains thereupon provided, shall cease '[2]—the words, it will be noted, implying that, notwithstanding the ordinance of 1326, a staple mart or staple marts continued to exist beyond the Channel. The statute of 1328.

This statute of 1328, which professed to abolish the staple system, such as it was, altogether, was apparently short-lived, for between 1328 and 1353 we read of the staple being moved from place to place on the other side of the water ;[3] while in 1337 the exportation of wools from England was for the moment wholly prohibited, the use of foreign cloth in England was prohibited, and the importation of foreign cloth into England was prohibited, foreign

[1] See Rymer.

[2] 2 Edw. III, cap. 9.

[3] See Rymer (Record Edition) under dates 10 February 1337, 12 November 1338, 8 August 1341, 26 November 1347, 5 April 1348, 1 December 1348. Anderson (*ut sup.*, vol. i, pp. 166, 172, 179, 184) says that in 1337 the staple was moved from Flanders to Brabant; that in 1341 it was re-established at Bruges; that in 1348 it was fixed at Calais, which had been taken in the preceding year ; and that in 1353 it was moved from Bruges to English towns by the statute of the staple. Rymer is quite explicit as to the staple being established at Bruges in 1341, a mayor and constables being appointed in the first instance by the king, their successors to be elected by the merchants. It seems clear, too, that it was established at Calais in 1348.

clothmakers being at the same time assured of protection in England and of being granted 'franchises
as many and such as may suffice them '.[1] The
object of the Government, in short, in this year was
to stimulate clothmaking in England at the expense
of the export trade in wool. There was no con-
sistent or continuous policy; but, whatever was or
was not ordained by king or Parliament, it is
obvious that, whenever wool was bought and sold,
there must have been central markets to meet the
convenience of those who wished to buy or sell;
and even when, from 1353 onwards, there was more
semblance of a system, the establishment of certain
towns as staple towns on one side of the Channel
must—in spite of legal provision to the contrary—
have involved supplementary centres on the other
side, as feeders of or receivers from the official
staple marts.[2]

The
Statute
of the
Staple,
1353.

The great Act of Parliament known as the Statute
of the Staple, or the Ordinance of the Staples, was
passed in the year 1353.[3] It provided that the

---

[1] 11 Edw. III, caps. 1-5.

[2] Thus Anderson (i. 184), in noting that in 1353 the staple was
moved from Bruges to English towns, says, 'Yet Calais still remained
as a staple'. Archdeacon Cunningham (*ut sup.*, pp. 622-4) gives
a document of the year 1359, in which King Edward III modified the
staple rules in favour of English merchants at Bruges, this royal
recognition of these merchants being followed by a licence to them
to elect a governor. This seems practically to amount to (*a*) the
recognition of some kind of staple centre at Bruges, in spite of the
staple being at the time by law fixed in England, and (*b*) an early stage
in the rise of the Merchant Adventurers. (See below, pp. 59, 61 notes.)

[3] 27 Edw. III, stat. ii.

staple of wools, leather, woolfels and lead [1] should be held at certain places within the realm and nowhere else.   For England, Newcastle-upon-Tyne, York, Lincoln, Norwich, Westminster, Canterbury, Chichester, Winchester, Exeter, and Bristol were named as staple towns; for Wales, Caermarthen; for Ireland, Dublin, Waterford, Cork, and Drogheda. To York, Lincoln, Norwich, Westminster, Canter· bury, and Winchester, not being ports themselves, the following ports respectively were assigned : Hull, Boston (then called St. Botolph's or St. Botolph's town), Great Yarmouth, London, Sandwich, and Southampton.   To these centres the wool was to be brought prior to export : here the sacks were to be weighed and sealed with the seal of the mayor of the staple ; and at the ports the customs duties were to be paid.   Alien, as well as denizen, merchants might buy the staple products at will throughout the land, provided that they brought them to the staples ; but aliens alone might export, being bound by an oath to hold no second staple beyond the seas.   It was made a felony for the king's subjects to export, or to take any part whatever, direct or indirect, in the sale beyond the seas.

The machinery which the statute created for

---

[1] It will be noted that tin does not appear among the staple articles, and in the ordinance of 1369 lead drops out also ; but later again, in 1378, 2 Ric. II, stat. i, cap. 3, tin comes in again, and by one reading of the statute lead also.

carrying its provisions into effect consisted of a mayor and two constables : the first appointments were to be made by the king, but the successors were to be elected by 'the commonalty of the merchants of the said places', the commonalty including aliens as well as British subjects.   A certain number of experienced men of good standing were to be appointed as 'correctors', before whom buyers and sellers might, if they wished, register their bargains.   Alien merchants were specially protected by a provision that they should choose two of their number to be assessors to the mayor and constables in cases in which aliens were concerned ;[1] and a board of six arbitrators was constituted to settle disputes arising between buyer and seller as to quality or weight of wool, two of them being Germans, two Lombards, and two English.   Very full and extensive powers were given to the mayor and constables of the staples. They were entrusted with 'jurisdiction and cognisance within the towns where the staples shall be,

---

[1] Cap. 24, the words run: 'That the merchants strangers shall choose two merchants strangers, whereof the one towards the South, and the other towards the North, shall be assigned to sit with the mayor and constables of the staples, where [some] of those persons chosen shall come, to hear the plaints touching merchants aliens, that shall be moved before the mayor and constables, at all times that any of the said persons chosen will be there, and to see that plain right be done to the said merchants aliens.' Apparently there was one assessor for the North of England, and one for the South, who came to the staple towns to sit only when there were important cases affecting alien merchants.

of people, and of all manner of things touching the
staple'.[1]   The law applied on all points relating to
the staple was to be the law merchant, not the
common law of the land or the customs of the
towns.   The judges of the realm and their officers
were excluded from the sphere of the mayor of the
staple,[2] to whom the mayor of the town in which
the staple was planted was, with his subordinates,
required to give every help.   Special houses and
streets were to be appointed for storing the staple
goods, and there was even to be a special prison
for those convicted in the court of the mayor of the
staple.[3]

The Statute of the Staple is spoken of in modern
books as a consolidating ordinance ; and, so far as
there was any staple system, it must be interpreted
from this statute.   Apart from the machinery, which
was not so much created for the first time as
developed out of pre-existing rudiments, the two
main features of the law were, on the one hand,

[1] Cap. 8.

[2] The judicial powers given to the mayors, constables, and justices
of the staple by the statute were very extensive, including criminal
jurisdiction.   By a later statute of 1362, 36 Edw. III, cap. 7, their
powers were confined to civil cases, contracts, &c., and criminal
jurisdiction was taken away from them.   'Process of felonies, and all
other pleas, as well within the staple as without, shall be at the
Common Law, as they were before the Statute of the Staple, notwithstanding the said statute.'

[3] For an account of the system established by the Statute of the
Staple, see Macpherson, *Annals of Commerce*, 1805, vol. i, pp. 546-50;
Gross, *The Gild Merchant*, 1890, vol. i, pp. 143-4 ; *The Cely Papers,*
ut sup., Introduction, p. ix.

Constant changes of policy.

that aliens alone should export ; on the other hand, that the staple markets should be held within the realm and on this side the Channel, at certain places alone, which were designated in the law. But these two outstanding provisions only held good for a very short while. In four years' time, in 1357,[1] British subjects were allowed for a while to export wool : again they were allowed in 1360-1.[2]

Changes in the provision forbidding British subjects to export wool.

In 1363-4 [3] the penalty of death provided by the Statute of the Staple for denizens guilty of the crime of exporting was abolished, but the other penalties were left in force ; and in 1369 [4] denizens who exported were made liable to forfeiture of the goods and three years' imprisonment. In 1390,[5] in Richard II's reign, denizens were forbidden to export ; but, when we come down to the reign of Edward IV, we find a law of the year 1463 [6] forbidding aliens to export, the object being to keep the bulk of the wool in England ' to the intent that sufficient plenty of the said wools may continually abide and remain within the said realm, as may competently and reasonably serve for the occupation of clothmakers '. By this date, though the statute upheld the wool staple at Calais, and allowed wool from the northern counties to be shipped at New-

[1] 31 Edw. III, stat. i, caps. 8-9. This Act in part revived the provisions of the ordinance of 1326.

[2] 34 Edw. III, cap. 21.

[3] 38 Edw. III, stat. i, caps. 2 and 6.

[4] 43 Edw. III, cap. 1.   [5] 14 Ric. II, cap. 5.

[6] 3 Edw. IV, cap. 1.

castle-upon-Tyne for other markets than Calais, English cloth was gaining the ascendancy over English wool and demanding the wool for home manufacture.

Even more frequent and more kaleidoscopic were the changes in the places where the staple markets might by statute or ordinance or royal pleasure be held. Ten years passed from the date when the great statute was enacted, and then, in 1363, the staple was moved to Calais. 'The same year', writes Stow, 'the staple of wool (notwithstanding the King's oath and other great estates) was ordained to be kept at Callis, and six and twenty marchants, the best and wealthiest of all England, to be farmers there, both of the town and staple, for three years. . . . He ordained there also two mayors, one for the town and one for the staple.'[1]

Changes in the staple markets.

Six years later, in 1369, under stress of war with France and in order to avoid danger to transport in the Channel, a law was passed providing that the staple at Calais should, to quote the quaint phrase,

---

[1] Stow (Kingsford, *ut sup.*), vol. ii, p. 103. It is clear, apart from Stow's statement, that the move was made to Calais in 1363, for the preamble to the statute of 43 Edw. III (1369) runs, 'Whereas of late it was advised for the profit of the realm, and ease of merchants of England, that the staple of wools, woolfels and leather should be holden at Calais, and there it hath been since the first day of March, the seven and thirtieth year of our Lord the King,' &c. (1363). Yet by 38 Edw. III, stat. i, cap. 7 (1363–4), 'It is assented that the staple shall be in England', and the Statute of the Staple was confirmed. The statute 2 Hen. VI, cap. 4 (1423) recites, 'Whereas the noble King Edward III did ordain his staple to be at Calais', and the marginal note refers to 36 Edw. III, i.e. 1362.

' be wholly put out '.[1] The staple was accordingly
moved back across the water. The same towns in
Ireland and Wales were named for staple centres
as had been named in the Statute of the Staple,
and the centres in England were for the most part
the same, the English staple towns under the new
law being Newcastle-upon-Tyne, Kingston-upon-Hull,
Boston, Yarmouth, Queenborough, Westminster,
Chichester, Winchester, Exeter, and Bristol. They
were ten in number, as before ; but Queenborough
was substituted for Canterbury with its port of
Sandwich, while Hull, Boston, and Yarmouth, which
in the former statute had figured only as the ports
of York, Lincoln, and Norwich, now supplanted
these three cities. Two ports only were left, as
serving adjacent staple markets, London for Westminster, and Southampton for Winchester. The
changes must obviously have been unpopular in the
displaced centres. Stow's account is that ' in the
44 of Edward the third Quinborough, Kingston
upon Hull, and Boston were made staples of wool,
which matter so offended some, that in the 50 of
his reign, in a parliament at London, it was com-
plained that the staple of wool was so removed
from Callis to diverse towns in England, contrary
to the statute appointing that citizens and marchants
should keep it there '.[2] The complaints seem to
have borne fruit, for in this 50th year of the reign,

[1] 43 Edw. III, cap. 1.
[2] Kingsford, *ut sup.*, vol. ii, pp. 103-4.

not by law but by royal grant dated the 23rd July, 1376, the staple went back to Calais.   Two years The staple at Calais. later, in 1378, its continuance at Calais was assured by a statute of Richard II.[1]   Ten years later again, however, in 1388,[2] we find a statute ordaining that the staple should be removed from Middelburg to Calais, from which it appears that in the interval the market had gone out of the realm altogether into Zeeland.   After another two years, in 1390,[3] we have a statute removing the staple into England, to be held at the places named in the Statute of the Staple; and yet again, while Richard II was still king, in 1397-8,[4] a law was passed providing that no licences should be allowed for exporting staple merchandises except to Calais, from which it would seem that by this date the staple had found its way back to Calais.   From this time onward Calais seems to have been more or less its permanent home; ordinances and statutes of the three Henrys (IV, V, and VI) and of Edward IV confirmed it there;[5] and it was the staple town

---

[1] 2 Ric. II, stat. i, cap. 1. Cf. Rymer under dates 23 July 1376, 16 December 1376, and 28 July 1377.

[2] 12 Ric. II, cap. 16. In Rymer, under date 3 September 1388, will be found mention of the governor of the staple at Middelburg. The charter given by Queen Elizabeth to the staplers in 1561, which is noticed below, p. 48, speaks of the staple having been removed from Middelburg to Calais.

[3] 14 Ric. II, cap. 1.

[4] 21 Ric. II, cap. 17.

[5] See 2 Hen. VI, cap. 4 (1423), which recites previous acts and ordinances; 3 Edw. IV, cap. 1 (1463), and 4 Edw. IV, caps. 2, 3 (1464-5).

par excellence, until it passed back into French hands, in the reign of Queen Mary, in the year 1558.

Importance of Calais.

Calais had been taken by Edward III in 1347, six years before the date of the Statute of the Staple. It was a most valuable prize, giving to the English a port from which English shipping had been sorely pirated, and with it control of the Straits of Dover. Its neighbourhood to and kinship with the Flemish towns, the main customers for English wool, marked it out as the place of all others where the wool staple could be most conveniently held, without moving the staple outside the realm. *The Cely Papers* give the correspondence of a family of merchants of the staple in the late years of the fifteenth century.[1] They had a London home and place of business in Mark Lane—the Mart Lane, in St. Olave's parish, and there was a resident partner in Calais. The wool came mainly from the Cotswolds, Cotswold wool being of high repute;[2] it was weighed at Leadenhall;

---

[1] See *The Cely Papers* (*ut sup.*). Stow (Kingsford, i. 132; see also ii. 289) speaks of monuments in St. Olave's Church, Hart Street, to ' Richard Cely and Robert Cely felmongers, principal builders and benefactors of this church'. The monuments are not in existence now. In *The Paston Letters*, which are of much the same date as *The Cely Papers*, will be found a letter from Sir John Paston of 30 June 1476, in which he comments on the difficulty of getting money out of the hands of Merchants of the Staple (*The Paston Letters*, edited by James Gairdner, 1875, vol. iii, p. 166).

[2] Thus Rymer gives an entry in 1438 of sixty sacks of Cotswold wool being allowed to be exported for the King of Portugal, and it is referred to in *The Libel of English Policy*.

and the ships which carried it to Calais hailed from all the Eastern and South-eastern ports from Boston to the Medway. Presumably the Cely family were typical of English wool-merchants generally, shipping to this staple centre; and yet the monopoly which was given to Calais as a market for the staple wares of England was after all but a limited monopoly, and was indifferently maintained. Royal licences seem to have been given from the time of Richard II onward to the citizens of Newcastle-upon-Tyne to export staple produce from the northern counties elsewhere than to Calais : there is a statute of Henry VI, in the year 1429, temporarily taking away these licences ; and in Edward IV's reign, if not before, the Newcastle privileges were established by law.[1] Again Calais was the staple for Flanders

Excep-tions to the monopoly of the Calais wool staple.

[1] See Anderson, i. 288. A statute of 1423 (2 Hen. VI, cap. 4) confirmed and renewed previous ordinances and statutes prescribing that staple merchandises should be sent to Calais only, but made an exception in favour of the wool, fells and leather of the four northern counties, Northumberland, Westmoreland, Cumberland, and the bishopric of Durham, without specifying Newcastle as their shipping port. A statute of 1429 (8 Hen. VI, cap. 21) repealed all licences to the men of Newcastle and Berwick to export staple merchandises elsewhere than to Calais. A statute of 1463 (3 Edw. IV, cap. 1) provided that wool and woolfels should be carried to Calais only, but excepted the wools of the four northern counties and the counties of Alderton (Northallerton) and Richmond, providing that this northern wool should be shipped at Newcastle only. A statute of 1464-5 (4 Edw. IV, caps. 2, 3) provided that wool should be shipped at certain specified English ports only and carried to Calais only, but again excepted the four northern counties, Richmondshire and Northaldertonshire, whose wool was to be shipped at Newcastle ' to pass at their liberty, this act notwithstanding '. It is perfectly clear that for the North of England Newcastle was put in the place of Calais, and that wool shipped at

and Northern Europe only. Staple goods for the Mediterranean, for the markets of Genoa or Venice, were not sent to Calais at all, but were shipped direct from England, mainly, if not wholly, from the port of Southampton. In 1378, in Richard II's reign,[1] while it was provided by law, as we have seen, that the staple should be held at Calais, it was at the same time provided by law that the merchants of the West, as they were termed, the 'merchants of Genoa, Venice, Catalonia, Arragon, and of other realms, lands, and countries towards the West', might buy for their own markets staple merchandises of England at 'Hampton or elsewhere within the realm', instead of going to Calais for them, and later ordinances and statutes contained similar provisions.

As has already been suggested, it can hardly be supposed that the removal of the staple to Calais involved the complete extinction of the staples in the English cities.[2] The cities concerned were too many and too strong to have acquiesced in total

Newcastle need not be sent to Calais. Mr. Malden seems to be mistaken in writing that the staple products from these northern districts 'were to go to Newcastle and thence to Calais only' (*The Cely Papers*, Introduction, pp. viii, ix).

[1] 2 Ric. II, stat. i, cap. 3. See also 2 Hen. V, stat. ii, cap. 6 (1414); 2 Hen. VI, cap. 4 (1423), &c. See Anderson, i. 257; Macpherson, i. 587-8.

[2] A statute of 1427 (6 Hen. VI, cap. 6) provided that every merchant, denizen and alien, should be allowed to ship goods at Melcombe in Dorset, for Calais. This seems to imply that only certain English ports might ship goods to the staple at Calais. In this law denizens and aliens are on the same footing.

abolition of the profit which accrued to a recognized wool market. Bitter enough feeling was caused when one English town supplanted another in this respect, as when the staple was moved from York to Hull and from Lincoln to Boston; and it is impossible to believe that all the staples in England were at once and summarily closed down in favour of Calais. Probably the Calais market became more exclusively the one market for Flemish buyers of English wool, as the wool became used more and more in England, as the export of wool grew less and less, and therefore as the advantage of being a staple town gradually died away; but in the fourteenth century and the first half of the fifteenth century to be a staple town meant much.

'The erecting of the staple for wool at Westminster', we are told, 'occasioned so great a resort to that royal village, that it thereby grew up to a pretty good town.'[1]   The site of the Westminster wool staple apparently was near where Bridge Street now runs; the jurisdiction of the mayor of the staple extended from Temple Bar to Tothill Fields;[2] and in view of the great amount of wool which passed through the Westminster market and was shipped at the Port of London, the mayor of the Westminster staple was paid £100 per annum, and

The Westminster wool staple.

[1] Anderson, i. 184.
[2] By 28 Edw. III, cap. 15 (1354), ' It is accorded and established that the staple of Westminster shall begin his bound at Temple Bar and extend to Tutehill '.

each of the two constables 10 marks per annum.[1]

[1] By the ordinance of the fees of the mayors and constables of the staple, either 1353 or 1354, 27 or 28 Edw. III, 'The mayor of the staple of Westminster shall take C li (£100) and every of the constables there ten marks'. Ten marks represented £13 6s. 8d.; but another reading of the statute is, 'and every of the constables there twenty Pounds'. The preamble of the ordinance runs, 'And now cometh as much wools, or well nigh as much, to the port of London, as do in all the other staples through the realm': the mayor of the Westminster staple was accordingly paid more highly than any other mayor of a staple. For an account of the Woolstaple at Westminster see Strype, ut sup., vol. ii, Bk. VI, pp. 6, 7. The writer says of the court of the mayor of the staple at Westminster, 'This court, though it were far more ancient, was strengthened and warranted by Act of Parliament, 27 Edw. III'. A notification of the election of the mayor and two constables of the Westminster staple in 1358 is given in *English Economic History, Select Documents, ut sup.*, p. 184. Anderson (i. 206) says, on Rymer's authority, that in 1375 the staple was removed from Westminster; he suggests, to Staple Inn. Elsewhere (p. 125) he says, 'The Inn of Chancery near Holborn Bars is so denominated from their warehouses anciently there situated'. Staple Inn, however, does not seem to have had any special connexion with the Company of the Staple or the Westminster staple. It was simply a stapled hall, or wholesale warehouse, until it became an Inn of Chancery (see Kingsford's ed. of Stow, ii. 363). On the other hand, in a petition to Edward VI, in or about 1551, the staplers refer to ' the place called the Staple Inn ' as having been their property, but it is not clear whether this was at Calais or in London (*S. P. Dom. Ed. VI*, vol. xiii, No. 80). By King Edward IV's charter to the citizens of London of 1463, 'The tonnage, and weighing, and measuring, laying up, and placing, and housing of whatsoever wools, by whomsoever, from whatsoever parts, brought or to be brought to the city aforesaid, which have beforetime been accustomed to be brought to the staple at Westminster, shall from hence be, and be made in the place called Leadenhall, within our city aforesaid, and in no other place within three miles of the said city '. This seems to mean that the staple was moved from Westminster to Leadenhall in the city of London at that date (see Maitland's *History of London*, 1756 (vol. i, p. 204). The court of the mayor of the staple, however, still existed at Westminster in Coke's time. See Coke upon Littleton, 1809 ed., vol. vii, pp. 237–8, cap. xlvi, on The Court of the Mayor of the Staple.

King Henry VI was said to have had six wool houses at Westminster, which he granted to the dignitaries of St. Stephen's Church; and possibly the decline of the staple may be traced in the licence, given in Rymer under the date 10 June 1529, to the dean of St. Mary and St. Stephen's Westminster to demolish and re-edify the ruinous tenements in the Wool Staple. Other towns and ports thrived, like Westminster, on their staple privileges, but what their status was after the staple had been moved to Calais is quite uncertain.

The staplers figure in a Proclamation for a free mart at Calais, which was issued by Henry VII in January 1505, and to which further reference will be made.[1] The Proclamation more especially concerned the Merchant Adventurers, who were for the time translated from the Low Countries to Calais, and who had become a strong, and were becoming a well-defined, company. It bore witness to the rivalry between the older and the younger organization, for it contained provisions to regulate their mutual relations. Gerard Malynes asserts that in the thirty-sixth year of King Henry VI, in 1457–8, that king gave the staplers a charter, in which it was stated that Henry IV's charter to the Merchant Adventurers was 'not meant to trouble or disquiet the Merchants of the Staple in bodies or goods in

The Staplers and the Merchant Adventurers at Calais. The Proclamation of 15 Jan. 1505.

---

[1] See below, p. 70. The Proclamation will be found in the volume *S. P. Dom. Charles II*, 1661, vol. xxvii.

the Low Countries '.[1] Similarly, Henry VII was
at pains to keep the peace between them when they
were brought into close quarters with each other at
Calais. The Proclamation provided that the sale
of the Merchant Adventurers' wares at the Calais
mart was not to be hindered by the mayor and
fellowship of the staple. Cases 'concerning the
feat of Merchants Adventurers' were to be tried
before the governor or governors and fellowship of
the Adventurers : cases 'concerning the feat of
Merchants of the Staple' before the mayor of the
staple. 'Every Merchant of the Staple using or
exercising the said feat of Merchant Adventurers
buying and bartering any of the said merchandises
belonging unto the same feat [was] not only [to]
observe and keep the statutes and ordinances made
or to be made and ordained from time to time by
the said Merchants Adventurers, but also be con-
tributors unto them for the same like as others
Merchants Adventurers do or hereafter ought to do.'
A corresponding provision safeguarded the staplers
in turn, if Merchant Adventurers entered into their
line of business. It is clear that by this date the
staplers were developing into a company in the
ordinary sense. The elaborate system which had
been embodied in the Statute of the Staple had
gradually become obsolete : the staple had been for
a long time domiciled at this one port of Calais ;
and the merchants, who had been part and parcel

---

[1] *The Center of the Circle of Commerce (ut sup.)*, p. 94.

of a Government machinery, designed for all the staple industries of England, but especially for wool, were now little more than English merchants who dealt in wool, who had an organization modelled on old lines for that particular trade, and whose actual market was at Calais.

In or about the year 1551,[1] we find them petitioning King Edward VI on the state of their trade. It had decayed owing to the importation of Spanish wool, the constantly growing demand for English wool for home manufactures with a consequent decrease in the export, and the fact that alien merchants were not compelled to buy and ship their wool at Calais. The petitioners asked that the privileges which had been granted to the staplers by charter by the king's ancestors, and confirmed by himself, should be renewed, and they offered a payment of £1,000 spread over three years as the price of renewal. *The staplers in Edward VI's reign.*

The loss of Calais followed in 1558; and in 1560[2] they laid their case before Queen Elizabeth and her advisers, pleading the gravity of the misfortune which had befallen them, the loss of property, the fact that the laws which governed the trade, and which had been framed for the Calais mart, had become of none effect through the loss of the town, *The loss of Calais, and the petition to Queen Elizabeth in 1560.*

[1] *S. P. Dom. Edw. VI*, vol. xiii, No. 80; *Cal. S. P. Dom.*, 1547–80, p. 37. See above, p. 44 note.

[2] *S. P. Dom. Eliz.*, vol. xv, No. 50; *Cal. S. P. Dom.*, 1547–80, pp. 168–9.

and the consequent anarchy which prevailed in the wool industry. The remedy which they suggested was the legal incorporation of one united fellowship under the government of an elected mayor and two constables—the old machinery, the mayor to hold office for a year or less, the constables for three months or less, mayor and constables to have authority over the whole body of staplers, and that body to be styled 'the Mayor Constables and Fellowship of Merchants of the Staple of England'. The fellowship were to be at liberty to hold their meetings in London or elsewhere; and, with a view to prospective marts in Flanders and Brabant, they asked 'to be exempted from the government rule or punishment of the governor of the Merchant Adventurers Trafficking into the Low Countries'.

The charter of 1561. The Queen acceded to the petition and granted them a charter on the 30th of May, 1561.[1] By this charter they were given perpetual succession and made a body corporate under the title which had been suggested, 'the Mayor Constables and Fellowship of the Merchants of the Staple of England'. The fellowship were to enjoy the privileges which they had enjoyed at Calais: the mayor and the two constables were to be the machinery of government: the meetings were to be held at

[1] Patent Rolls, 3 Eliz. Carr (*Select Charters of Trading Companies, 1530–1707*, Selden Society, 1913, p. xxi note) says that this charter was 'apparently given to avoid consequences of non-user during a recent period of disturbed trade'; but it seems rather to have been granted in order to embody the staplers as an up-to-date company.

will in London or elsewhere, and there were to be
three staple marts in the Low Countries—at Bruges
for Flanders, Middelburg for Zeeland, and Bergen
op Zoom for Brabant, or at any of them, as the
majority should determine, from which they were
not to be compulsorily moved except after nine
months' notice: they were licensed to sell wool
grown in England and to export it from all the
usual English ports.

Some kind of supplementary charter seems to have The
been given in 1584 ;[1] and the main grant was charter
of 1618.
renewed and confirmed by King James I in a new
charter which he gave to the staplers on the 29th of
March 1618.[2] Three years previously, in 1615,
when incorporating the new company of 'the
King's Merchants Adventurers of the New Trade
of London', King James had been careful to safeguard the staplers' rights. It will be seen later [3]
that this new company, designed to supplant the
Merchant Adventurers of England, proved a complete failure, and that the Merchant Adventurers
regained all of and more than their former privileges in a new charter of January 1618. In this
new charter again due provision was made to
protect the staplers, but it may be taken that they

[1] See *Cal. S. P. Dom.*, 1581-90, p. 202, under date 18 September
1584. Malynes speaks of two charters being given to the staplers by
Queen Elizabeth, 3rd and 26th Eliz. (*The Center of the Circle of Commerce*, 1623, p. 92).

[2] Patent Rolls, 15 Jac. I, Pt. VI, No. 4.

[3] See below, pp. 98-100.

in turn were given a charter for themselves as a set-off to the grant to the Merchant Adventurers.

This charter of King James in some sort seemed to revive the old order which Edward III had called into existence, by prescribing that the staple of wools and skins should, after the requisite nine months' notice had expired, be removed from the towns in the Low Countries, and that thenceforward the staple of wools and woolfels should be held within the realm and nowhere else. A large number of cities and towns were specified. London (the city of London and suburbs), Canterbury, Exeter, Norwich, Lincoln, Winchester savoured of the old time, and other towns, representing their respective counties, were named, such as Woodstock for Oxfordshire, Cirencester for Gloucestershire, Kendal for Westmoreland.[1] In all these places and elsewhere within the realm the fellowship were given full power, without hindrance from the king's officers, to deal with all kinds of wool. For the rest the king, professing his wish to restore the former prosperity of the staplers and to revive the wool trade, granted them no less privileges than before. The mayor, constables, and fellowship, meeting 'in the place called Leddenhall' in London,

---

[1] The other towns were Worcester, Shrewsbury and Oswestry for Salop, Northampton and Brackley for Northamptonshire, Reading for Berks., Sherborne for Dorset, Devizes for Wilts., Taunton (called Taunton Dean) for Somersetshire, Ratsdale (Rochdale) for Lancashire, Richmond, Wakefield, and Halifax for Yorkshire, Coggeshall for Essex.

or elsewhere, were to decide the rule and government of all the staplers in all the counties, who
were to be subordinate to their control.   A proviso,
however, was inserted, that the grant was not to
be in restraint of the trade of the clothworkers or
spinners of England.

In spite of references to privileges having been
confirmed by charter by previous kings, there does
not seem to have been any charter before the
charter of Elizabeth which can be said to have
incorporated the staplers as a company.   On these
two charters of Elizabeth and James they relied
in after years, as they sank into decay.   They had
gradually grown to be a company : rivalry with
the Merchant Adventurers crystallized them into
a company ; and when they were ousted from
Calais, it was only by taking definite form and
shape as a company that they could continue in
existence at all.   Queen Elizabeth did for them
what she did for the Merchant Adventurers, as we
shall see later.   She gave them a legal standing,
made them a corporate body ; and, as in the case
of the Merchant Adventurers, from having been
the merchants of the staple at Calais, they took on
a more national guise and the title of Merchants
of the Staple of England.   Evidently the seat of
government was to be in London—all the more so
when King James put an end to the wool staples
in the Low Countries.

Very interesting, characteristically English in

adherence to old forms and methods, is the fact
that the mayor and constables survived as the
machinery of government, and that English towns
were named as staple markets, as though to call
back into life the system of the Middle Ages.
What was actually in being was a society of wool
merchants, representing what remained of an export
trade which had once surpassed all others ; and
these charters, granted to the wool merchants
themselves, coupled with the clauses in charters
granted to other companies, which protected the
rights of the staplers, kept the latter alive after
their time of active usefulness had passed.

The rivalry between the staplers and the Merchant Adventurers. It may almost be said that they were indirectly
kept alive by the rival organization to which they
owed their downfall. The enemies of the Merchant
Adventurers were the friends of the staplers, and
were at pains to emphasize the staplers' claims
and to try to galvanize the staplers back into life,
as against the powerful company whose monopoly
was so well organized and so aggressive. The
champions of the staplers were of the class of men
who prefer the old to the new ; they regarded the
Merchant Adventurers as usurpers, they believed
that there might still be a future for the export

Gerard Malynes. trade in wool. In 1622 and 1623 Gerard Malynes,
commercial theorist or political economist of the
day, great on the subject of exchanges, took up
the cudgels on their behalf, and belaboured the
Merchant Adventurers and their advocate, Edward

Missenden, contending that the staplers had in
past times been exporters of cloth as well as of
wool, and that through the Adventurers' machina-
tions their activities had been restricted to the wool
trade. The controversy raged as to whether, when
staplers exported cloth, they had done so in their own
right or in virtue of being Merchant Adventurers
also, and Malynes contended that in the reigns of
Richard II, Henry VI, Edward IV, and Henry VII
'above an hundred mere staplers not free of the
Merchants Adventurers'[1] had shipped woollen
cloths to foreign parts in addition to similar shippings in the reigns of Henry VIII and Elizabeth.
As in the beginning staplers and Merchant Adventurers had been one and the same body of
merchants, so in later times the fact that individual
merchants belonged to both companies[2] made it
difficult to determine where the line should be
drawn between them.

There is an historical interest attaching to the
controversy. It is a useful reminder that the
merchants of the staple were in their origin not
merchants for wool alone but for all of what were
held to be the staple merchandises of England.
It was only because wool proved to be by far the

[1] *The Center of the Circle of Commerce*, 1623, p. 94. See above,
p. 13 note.

[2] The Merchant Adventurers did not relish having staplers as
members of their body, to judge by the fact that in or about 1580
they put forward reasons against the admission of any merchant of
the staple into their fellowship. See *Cal. S.P. Dom.*, 1547–80, p. 698.

most important of these merchandises that the
staple became in effect the wool staple, and the
merchants of the staple the wool merchants.
The old statutes and ordinances connected with the
staple, as has been seen, specified not only wool
and woolfels, but leather, lead, and tin 'and all
other merchandises pertaining to the staple';[1] and
then there arose the question whether cloth was
a staple merchandise, and whether the staplers
were justified in exporting it.   About the year
1583[2] they seem, at the suit of the Merchant

---

[1] 2 Hen. VI, cap. 4, 'the whole repair of wools, woolfels, leather,
lead [whole tin and] shotten tin, and all other merchandises pertaining to the staple'.

[2] See *Cal. S. P. Dom.*, 1581–90, pp. 78, 114, 637. On p. 637 is an
entry of application made to the Council by the staplers in or about
1589, and of the Merchant Adventurers' answer, 'points to prove that
cloths are no staple merchandise '.   In this connexion it is interesting
to note the preamble of the Act quoted in the previous note, 2 Hen. VI,
cap. 4 (1423), 'Whereas the noble King Edward the Third did ordain
his staple to be at Calais, and that the whole repairs of wools, woolfels,
leather, lead, tin, butter, cheese, and other merchandise, except
woollen cloths, and red herring, passing out of the realm of England
and his lands of Wales and Ireland, and his town of Berwick on
Tweed, should be at the said town of Calais '.   While butter and
cheese are added to the list of standard staple merchandises, woollen
cloths are expressly excepted.   A reference to 21 Ric. II, cap. 17
(1397–8), will show that in that Act wools, woolfels, leather, lead, tin,
cheese, butter, and honey are given as the articles which were then
sent, or ought to be sent, to the staple at Calais, and out of them
wools, leather, woolfels, tin, and lead are specified as 'the great
merchandises', with regard to which the staple law was to be strictly
enforced.   In Henry VII's Proclamation for a Free Mart at Calais (see
above, p. 45, and below, p. 70) are the words, 'tin, leather, butter,
cheese, tallow, and lead called staple ware '.   Stow, in claiming that
the merchants of the staple were the oldest merchants of England (as
above, p. 22), adds, 'It seemeth . . . that all commodities of the realm

Adventurers, to have been definitely prohibited from doing so; and it is clear that the prohibition was strongly enforced when Malynes wrote his indignant protests and after the Merchant Adventurers had gained the whip-hand over King James I.

But the quarrel was only the flickering of the embers when the fire had nearly gone out. The staplers lived on indefinitely, but they lived in a comatose condition; for all practical purposes, after King James I's reign at the latest, they pass out of history.[1] Their story is the story of the beginning of English exports on any considerable scale, and of a system which was devised for the purpose. The main interest of the system lies in the fact that the Government worked through private merchants, and used them as machinery for State purposes.

Here is an early illustration of co-operation between State authority and private enterprise, which has been the greatest of all factors in the making of the British Empire. No other people than the English have developed so strongly, so

are staple merchandises by law and charter, as wools, leather, woolfels, lead, tin, cloth, &c.' (Kingsford, vol. ii, p. 104). The standard list was no doubt wool, woolfels, leather, lead, tin; and other articles were added at will from time to time.

[1] Anderson, writing in 1764, says (i. 125), 'At this day they are only a mere name, without any virtual existence; nevertheless they keep up the form and show of a corporation by continuing annually to elect the officers of their company as directed by their ancient charters,' &c. Macpherson has adopted a revised version of this passage in the case of the Eastlanders, below, p. 176.

illogically, and so successfully an understanding between private initiative and State control, and we see the beginning of it in the staple system. This system, in a most clumsy, shifting, uncertain way, none the less did its work; and, when its time was past, out of the system there emerged a company which appealed to the past as though it had always existed on company lines, and prolonged its existence partly by the feeling which was excited of tenderness for the past, and partly because the company was a useful rallying point against the monopoly of another company. But it was no more than the shell of a company, without the substance. What membership fees, if any, the staplers paid; what privileges the fees secured; what rules governed the fellowship; whether the mayor and constables in London exercised any real authority over any one else, is all to seek. Whatever the company was or did, it faded to nothing, overshadowed and obliterated by a rival and far more masterful association.

CHAPTER III

THE MERCHANT ADVENTURERS OF ENGLAND

In a pamphlet of or about the year 1670,[1] entitled 'The advantages of the Kingdom of England, both abroad and at home, by managing and issuing the drapery and woollen manufactures of this kingdom under the ancient government of the Fellowship of Merchant Adventurers of England', we read that 'In King Edward I's time, there did spring up out of the Guild of Mercers, London, a sort of English merchants, who first began to attempt the bringing in the making of cloth into this land, and about anno 1296[2] they obtained privileges of John II, Duke of Brabant, and stapled themselves in Antwerp, joining in society with them all other English merchants resorting to those parts'. The privileges given by the Duke of Brabant in 1296 were, as has

The origin of the Merchant Adventurers.

----

[1] B. M. 712. g. $\frac{16}{9}$.

[2] See the note to p. 22 above, in which Strype and Maitland are quoted as asserting that the Merchant Adventurers were incorporated by Edward I in 1296. Similarly, Burgon (*Life and Times of Sir Thomas Gresham*, 1839) says (vol. i, p. 187) that they were incorporated by Edward I as early as 1296, 'when they established a factory at Antwerp and employed themselves in the manufacture of woollen cloths'; though a few lines before he says, 'From the society known by the name of Merchants of the Staple arose in 1358 another, called the company of the Merchant Adventurers'.

been seen, given to English merchants generally, before they were divided into staplers and Merchant Adventurers. We have seen too that, like the staplers, the Merchant Adventurers claimed an ancient origin, styling themselves the Brotherhood of St. Thomas Becket. This sainted antiquity was cast in their teeth in later years by outsiders, who resented their monopoly and their exactions. This is shown by the preamble to the Act of 1496, with its references to the fines 'demanded by colour of a fraternity of St. Thomas of Canterbury' and to 'feigned holiness'. The Adventurers grew out of, or at any rate were very closely connected with, the Guild of Mercers, for down to 1526 the minutes of the two companies were kept in the same book, and prior to the great Fire of London in 1666, the Mercers' premises were the head-quarters of the London Merchant Adventurers.[1] In short, out of the municipal guild, and on the lines of the municipal guild, grew the company for trading beyond the seas.

[1] The source of this information appears to be the Mercers' Records. See the *Life and Typography of William Caxton*, 1861, by William Blades, pp. 13–16, and the authorities given on p. 13. The Merchant Adventurers had an office under the Mercers' Hall down to the date of the Fire of London. Mr. Blades shows that in early days the Mercers were predominant among the Merchant Adventurers, and this is proved by the wording of the preamble of the Act of 1496, which speaks of 'the fellowship of the Mercers and other merchants and Adventurers dwelling and being free within the City of London' (see below, p. 68). See also Dr. Dendy's *Extracts from the Records of the Merchant Adventurers of Newcastle-upon-Tyne*, Surtees Society, vol. i, 1895, Preface, p. xxxiv.

The account which their secretary, John Wheeler, writing in 1601, gave of their origin, is that they obtained privileges from the Duke of Brabant in 1248, being then the brotherhood of St. Thomas Becket of Canterbury; that in 1358, after Calais had been taken by the English, Louis, Earl of Flanders, gave large privileges to English merchants, and that the company, which had been recognized by the English king, Edward III, settled themselves at Bruges, whence they removed to Middelburg, and from Middelburg, about 1444, to Antwerp; that in 1446 Philip the Good, Duke of Burgundy, 'gave privileges' at Antwerp 'to the Company under the name of the English nation, by which name the said company ever since hath been most commonly known in the Low Countries',[1] and those privileges were confirmed in the same year by the city authorities. It can only be repeated that the fact that both the staplers and the Merchant Adventurers claimed the same origin, that both were reputed to have begun their trading operations outside the realm, in Brabant or Flanders,

---

[1] *A Treatise of Commerce, &c.*, by John Wheeler, secretary to the Merchants Adventurers, 1601, printed at Middelburg by the printer to the States of Zeeland, pp. 8, 9, 15, 17, another edition being printed in London at the same time. The statement that the company settled at Bruges in or after 1358, having been recognized by Edward III, seems to be borne out by the document of 1359 referred to above, p. 32 note. Rymer mentions in the years 1359, 1360, 1361 John Walewayn, who was much employed by Edward III, and who is styled 'governor of the merchants at Bruges' and 'governor of the merchants in Flanders'.

and that the same dates are given in either case, simply means that originally there was only one set of merchants, who subsequently parted into two bands. The staplers became the home merchants, mainly concerned with the export of the raw product, wool. The Merchant Adventurers became the English merchants domiciled or sojourning across the seas, in foreign parts though near home : they were concerned with importing into the cities and lands wherein they planted themselves, not wool grown in England, but cloth made in England from English wool.

The first charter of the Merchant Adventurers.

The staplers, however, had undoubted claim to seniority as against the Merchant Adventurers. The staplers could point to the reigns of Edward II and Edward III for laws or royal edicts, bearing undeniable evidence to their separate and concrete existence. The Merchant Adventurers, on the other hand, if the ordinary accounts are accepted, must be held to have dated officially only from the reign of Henry IV. ' In the year 1399,' says Wheeler, ' the art of making of cloth being grown to good perfection within this realm, King Henry IV first prohibited the invection of foreign made cloth, and gave unto the said company a very beneficial and ample charter of privileges, confirmed by Act of Parliament, for the same purpose and intent, as his predecessor King Edward the Third had done before him.'[1] The charter contained, we are told, a provision

[1] Wheeler, p. 9.

'that any man paying the haunce of an old noble
might freely consort and trade with them',[1] and it
was, we are told again more accurately, 'a charter
to govern this trade both abroad and at home, and
he (the king) grounded the same upon defect of
good government'.[2] In other words, the king gave
permission to the merchants, who constituted or
were the forerunners of the company, to choose a
governor with duly authorized powers.[3] The grant,

[1] See *A Discourse consisting of motives for the Enlargement and
Freedom of Trade, ut sup.*, 1645, p. 21. Quoted also by Anderson, i.
233, who makes an old noble equal to 'about 18/- of modern money'.

[2] From the pamphlet of 1670, quoted above on p. 57.

[3] The question of the first grant to the Merchant Adventurers is, or
was, somewhat obscure. As stated in the text, Wheeler says explicitly
that Henry IV gave a very 'ample charter', which was confirmed by
Act of Parliament, but there is no record of any such Act at this date.
The grant, which was the foundation of the statement of Wheeler and
other writers, is given in Rymer under date 5 February 1406/7, and
is a royal licence to the English merchants in Holland, Zeeland,
Brabant, and Flanders to elect governors and make laws and regulations for themselves. This grant or licence was magnified by those
who came after, as Macpherson points out in the following note
(*Annals of Commerce*, 1805, vol. i, p. 617, note) : 'This is the charter
by which the company of Merchant Adventurers claimed the exercise
of exclusive trade. But there is here no intention of any exclusive
privilege nor any hint of a corporate body, or a collective name,
whether of St. Thomas Becket or Adventurers. Wheeler, Misselden,
Malynes, and other keen disputants on both sides of those now
dormant contests, seem all to have asserted boldly without giving
themselves much trouble in searching for records to substantiate their
pretensions.' Anderson is confusing, for he notices grants under both
1406 and 1407 (vol. i, pp. 233-4). But, if this grant of 5 February
1407 is the basis for Wheeler's statement, it is difficult to see why the
beginning of the Merchant Adventurers should not be put further
back, as e.g. to the licence of Edward III to the merchants at Bruges
to elect governors of 1359, which has been noticed above, pp. 32, 59.
Archdeacon Cunningham says (p. 623) that the group of merchants at

which was apparently the basis for the statements which have been quoted, was dated 5 February 1407 or 1406 old style. Further reference will be made to it : it related entirely to the better government of the English merchants in the Low Countries, and only indirectly constituted a company, no mention being made of any membership fee or of any common name. The fact that it was found necessary to provide by royal edict for the maintenance of law and order among English merchants on the Continent proves that, by the beginning of the fifteenth century, the wool and cloth trade had attracted a large number of Englishmen into residence outside the realm.[1]

The charter of Edward IV.
The successors of Henry IV confirmed or extended this grant, notably Edward IV, whose voluminous new charter of the 16th of April 1462 will be found in Hakluyt.[2] It gave to the English merchants

Bruges in 1359 'occupied a position closely resembling that of the Merchant Adventurers fifty years later', but there does not seem any particular reason to distinguish them from the Merchant Adventurers, and possibly Wheeler may be referring to this 1359 grant when he says (pp. 8 and 9) that Edward III confirmed the privileges given in 1248 by John, Duke of Brabant 'for the substantial government of the said company in their trade', though Bruges of course was not in Brabant but in Flanders.

[1] For this and later charters given to the Merchant Adventurers see the charter of Charles II, which refers to or recites them all, except the charter of Edward IV. *S. P. Dom. Charles II*, 1661, January, vol. xxvii. There is some confusion in the recital of the old charters, but there were at least two grants by Henry V, in 1413 and 1420, and one by Henry VI on 20 June 1428.

[2] The charter is headed 'A large Charter granted by K Edward the 4 in the Second year of his reign, to the merchants of England

settled in Flanders, Hainault, Holland, Zeeland, permission to elect a governor with sufficient lieutenants and deputies and 'justicers' not exceeding twelve; but still the title of Merchant Adventurers had not come into use. Before this date, in 1446, while Henry VI was on the throne, the English merchants had, as we have learnt from Wheeler, secured a grant of new privileges from the then ruler of the Low Countries, Philip the Good, Duke of Burgundy,[1] a grant which was afterwards confirmed by the Intercursus Magnus of 1496.

The *Libel of English Policy*,[2] written about 1437, in Henry VI's reign, tells of the busy commerce of the Low Countries and of English trade with the Low Countries in the middle years of the fifteenth century. Incidentally it illustrates the constant use of the term 'staple':

> 'For Flanders is staple, as men tell me,
>   To all nations of Christianity.'

The Libel of English Policy.

resident especially in the Netherland, for their choosing of a master and governor among themselves, which government was first appointed unto one William Obray, with express mention what authority he should have' (Hakluyt, *ut sup.*, vol. ii, pp. 147–58). It is a wholly new charter making no reference to previous grants. Possibly for this reason it was omitted in the recitals contained in the charter of Charles II.

[1] It was a commercial treaty for twelve years signed at Calais 4 August 1446 (see Rymer). Great stress was laid upon it in *Articles offered to the Council by the Merchants Adventurers upon occasion of the treaty with the Dutch* (the date being given as the 6th of August), 3 November 1653 (Rymer).

[2] Hakluyt, *ut sup.*, vol. ii, pp. 114–47.

And Spain sent her products

'Unto Bruges, as to her staple fayre.'

The main English export was still evidently wool rather than cloth:

'But Flemings, if ye be not wroth,
The great substance of your cloth at the full
Ye wot ye make it of our English wool.'

Both Spain and Flanders largely depended, according to the writer, upon English commodities, wool and tin. English cloth is chiefly mentioned in connexion with Brabant:

'And we to martis in Brabant charged been
With English cloth full good and fair to seen.'

Bruges. Bruges was about this date the city which outshone all others, and Bruges was the first headquarters of the Merchant Adventurers, after they had begun to form a distinct body of traders. In after years they referred to it as 'the town of Bridges their most ancient residence in Flanders'.[1] Wheeler's account is that the citizens of Bruges turned against the Adventurers, who were forced to leave the city for Middelburg; that in or about 1444 'Antwerp, being but a poor and simple town, standing in Brabant, made great suit to the company'; that the Adventurers then went to Antwerp and made their chief centre there and at Bergen op

[1] From *A petition of the Merchant Adventurers concerning the removing their company from Rotterdam to Flanders* received by the Council of State, 4 November 1652 (Rymer).

Zoom ; [1] that the Antwerp connexion was temporarily severed by removal to Calais in the reign of Henry VII ; that from Calais they went back to Middelburg, and thence again to Antwerp, remaining at Antwerp until the final rupture between England and Spain.[2] It is almost impossible to follow the exact steps of the Adventurers, especially in these early years, but it would seem that they must have retained some kind of footing at Bruges later than the date given by Wheeler, for Bruges was the residence of a great Englishman, who was undoubtedly governor of the company—no less a man than William Caxton. Apprenticed to a mercer in 1438, and at a later date a full member of the Mercers' Guild, he went to Bruges in or about 1441. In 1462-3, after the grant of Edward IV's charter, he acted as governor of the Merchant Adventurers, and a little later was definitely appointed governor, being referred to in August 1464 as the 'governor beyond the sea'.[3] He spent thirty years and more in all in the Low Countries, and it was at Bruges that

William Caxton.

---

[1] With regard to Bergen op Zoom, Wheeler says on p. 138, ' Because the Hanses unmeasurably frequented the city of Antwerp with English commoditie, the Merchants Adventurers were forced to draw themselves wholly to the said city, and leave Bergen op Zoom, where they used to keep two marts in the year '.

[2] Wheeler (*ut sup.*), pp. 15-17.

[3] 16 August 1464 is the date given in Blades's *Life and Typography of William Caxton*, vol. i, p. 14. The *Dictionary of National Biography* gives 16 August 1465. While Caxton was governor, there was one of the periodical ruptures of trading relations between England and the Low Countries, which was after a while duly adjusted.

he governed the Merchant Adventurers, dwelling in the 'English house', the *Domus Anglorum*. He does not seem to have had any connexion with Antwerp, and it is difficult to reconcile the fact of his governorship with Wheeler's account of the removal of the Adventurers to Antwerp in the year 1444. It is certain, however, that Antwerp had become the head-quarters of the fellowship in the later years of the century.[1]

It was not till the days of the Tudor sovereigns that the company attained its majority, so to speak, and the name of Merchant Adventurers came into official use. By this time they had grown to maturity and strength, and had become a power in the State. The reign of Henry VII stands out prominently in their story, and very prominent figures were they in that reign—the reign which began the modern history of England, and in which John Cabot piloted Englishmen for the first time across the North Atlantic Ocean.

The Merchant Adventurers in the reign of Henry VII.

In its first year, on the 4th of February 1486, we have a petition to the king from the 'inhabitants, Merchant Adventurers, citizens of the city of London, into the parts of Holland, Zeeland, Brabant, and Flanders'. The petitioners called attention to the expenses which they had incurred in paying soldiers to guard their trade, and they also asked

The petition of 1486.

---

[1] Archdeacon Cunningham says that the Merchant Adventurers moved their factory from Bruges to Antwerp in 1494 (*Growth of English Industry and Commerce in Modern Times*, Pt. I, 1907, p. 224), but this must surely be a misprint.

for a rebate of dues which had been paid on imports
from the Low Countries into the river Thames and
the port of London, during the interval between the
first day of the reign and the meeting of Parliament,
inasmuch as such dues had not been legally authorized. They petitioned as Londoners, it will be
noted, as Merchant Adventurers of London, not yet
of England, as men who imported and exported by
the great waterway of the Thames. The petition
was granted, a good omen of coming relations with
the Crown.[1]

A few years passed, and there was trouble with
the Flemings. This was due to the countenance
given to Perkin Warbeck by the rulers of Flanders ;
for the Dowager Duchess of Burgundy, the Lady
Margaret, was of Yorkist blood and sympathy. In
1493 King Henry moved the head-quarters of the
company from Antwerp, where they were then
planted, to Calais, and drove the Flemings ' as well
their persons as their wares '[2] out of England. The
Flemings retaliated, and at this critical time the
Merchant Adventurers proved their resourcefulness
and their strength. ' The Merchant Adventurers ',
writes Bacon, ' being a strong company (at that
time) and well underset with rich men and good
order, did hold out bravely ; taking off the com-

The rup-
ture with
the Flem-
ings.

[1] For this petition see Campbell, *Materials for a History of the Reign
of Henry VII*, 1873, vol. i, p. 273, and Pollard, *The Reign of Henry VII
from Contemporary Sources*, 1913–14, vol. ii, p. 27.

[2] Bacon's *History of the Reign of King Henry VII*, Ellis and Spedding, 1870 ed., vol. vi, p. 147.

modities of the Kingdom, though they lay dead upon their hands for want of vent.'[1] He tells us also the sequel. Friendly relations with the Flemings were restored by the commercial treaty of 24th February 1496, the *Intercursus Magnus*,[2] and 'the English merchants came again to their mansion at Antwerp, where they were received with procession and great joy'.[1] In that same year, to quote Bacon again, 'there passed a law, at the suit of the Merchant Adventurers of England, against the Merchant Adventurers of London, for monopolizing and exacting upon the trade; which, it seemeth, they did a little to save themselves, after the hard time they had sustained by want of trade. But those innovations were taken away by Parliament.'[1]

The law of 1496.

The preamble to the law of 1496 [3] recited a petition on the part of 'The Merchant Adventurers inhabiting and dwelling in divers parts of this realm of England out of the city of London', protesting in bitter terms against the exactions which they alleged they had suffered at the hands of 'the Fellowship of the Mercers and other Merchants and Adventurers dwelling and being free within the City of London'. It was one of the periodical

[1] Bacon's *History of the Reign of King Henry VII* (*ut sup.*), pp. 172, 173, 175. As stated above, p. 65, Wheeler makes them go back to Middelburg and thence to Antwerp.

[2] The *Intercursus Magnus* is printed from Rymer in Pollard (*ut sup.*), vol. ii, pp. 285–309.

[3] 12 Hen. VII, cap. 6.

revolts of provincial traders and producers against
the domination of London. Evidently at this
date Londoners held the field in the Low Countries, and the Merchant Adventurers in the Low
Countries, so far as they were an organized body,
were Merchant Adventurers of London. The petitioners urged that elsewhere they were free to trade
without let or hindrance, to Spain, to Portugal,
to the Eastland countries and various other lands :
time was when they had been free also to trade to
Flanders, Holland, Zeeland, and Brabant, ' in which
places the universal marts be commonly kept and
holden four times in the year ' ; but the Merchants
of London had formed a confederacy to exclude all
Englishmen from these marts, unless they paid
a fine to the fellowship. This fine at first ' was but
the value of half an old noble sterling ' : afterwards
it was increased to 100 shillings Flemish ; and at
the date of the petition it stood at £20 sterling.[1]
The petition effected its object, in so far that the
law provided that no fine should be exacted beyond
the limit of ten marks sterling (£6 13s. 4d.) ; but
Parliament, by fixing a maximum, thereby legalized

[1] Froude (*History of England,* under date March 1553, chap. xxi,
1860 ed., vol. v, p. 469) speaks of the fine as having been raised to
£40, and this figure is also given in other books ; but the law specifies
clearly £20 as the maximum which had been reached. Froude speaks
of the monopolists as ' The Fellowship of the London Merchants ', and
the plaintiffs as ' The Merchant Adventurers or unattached traders ',
the truth being that both parties were Merchant Adventurers, but the
monopolists—the Londoners—were the lineal ancestors of the great
company in the direct line.

the right to levy a fine, and to that extent materially strengthened the position of the **Merchant Adventurers**.

Further troubles with the Flemings.

There was another interval of a few years after the *Intercursus Magnus* and the passing of this law, and then relations between England and Flanders were strained again. In consequence of alleged exactions in the Archdukes' countries, as the Low Countries were termed, King Henry, on the 15th of January 1505, issued a proclamation for a free mart at Calais, to be held every quarter for forty days. The mart was to be open to alien merchants as freely as to English, but all the trade between England and the Low Countries was to be handled at Calais alone, the proclamation being aimed against the Flemish marts. It was provided that the Merchant Adventurers should be corporate at Calais, as they had been in the Archdukes' countries, enjoying the same privileges as they had enjoyed at Antwerp. The governor of the fellowship was to have the same authority as in the Low Countries, and, as we have seen,[1] careful provision was made to prevent friction between the Adventurers and the Staplers, seeing that Calais was the Staplers' home and citadel.[2] The Proclamation was followed on the 28th of September 1505 by a new charter to the Merchant Adventurers.

Proclamation of a free mart at Calais.

[1] See above, pp. 45–6.

[2] This proclamation will be found in the volume containing the various charters of the company. *S. P. Dom. Charles II*, 1661, January, vol. xxvii.

This charter of Henry VII was addressed to the Merchant Adventurers at Calais. The term Merchant Adventurers now comes into formal use, but still they are not styled the Merchant Adventurers of England. Calais being their head-quarters at the time, at Calais they were authorized to hold their meetings; but a clause was inserted whereby their privileges would be safeguarded if they moved into countries in amity with England. As in the grant of Henry IV, so in this later charter, emphasis is laid on the evils arising from want of good government, and the charter is concerned not with monopoly of trade but with providing for good government by framing a constitution. The Adventurers were given authority to meet at Calais and elect a governor, and 'four and twenty of the most sad discreet and honest persons of divers fellowships of the said Merchants Adventurers' to be his assistants, thirteen to form a quorum. To the governor and his deputies, with the twenty-four assistants, was entrusted the power of making laws for the fellowship; whereas under the earlier grant of 1407 the laws were to be made by the governor 'by the common consent' of all the merchants. The laws were not to be contrary to the king's prerogative or to the diminution of the commonweal of the realm—a provision which reappears in later charters, but was absent from the charter of 1407. The membership fee was limited to ten marks sterling, as laid down by the law of 1496; while

the wording 'divers fellowships of the said Merchants Adventurers' may be taken as evidence that
the company was intended thenceforward to include
other groups of Adventurers besides Londoners, and
possibly as indicating that at this date the Merchant
Adventurers' fellowship was constituted rather as a
federation of groups of merchants at different city
centres than as a single fellowship.[1]

Letters
Patent of
24 Janu-
ary 1506. But the one great object of the charter was better
government, and this is the theme of further Letters
Patent, issued less than five months later, on the
24th of January 1506.[2]   The governor at the time,
John Sheldon, is referred to by name, and the
company is spoken of as 'our well-beloved subjects, the Merchant Adventurers of this our realm,
haunting our town of Calais and the Archdukes'
countries', from which it would seem that the
fellowship was already gravitating back to Flanders.
The company is stated to have fallen of late years
into great decay 'for lack and default of politic
rules and guiding among themselves', and especially
through the negligence and disobedience of the
members 'in not coming to their Assemblies and
Congregations limited and appointed for the order
and direction of their Commonweal'.   The whole
object of the document is to strengthen the hands
of the governor and his deputies in calling meetings

[1] This charter is reprinted in Appendix I to *The Early Chartered
Companies*, 1296–1858, Cawston and Keane, 1896, pp. 249–54.
[2] These Letters Patent are given in the 1661 volume (*ut sup.*).

of the fellowship and punishing members for non-attendance.

In this same January in which these Letters Patent were granted, the ruler of the Low Countries, the Archduke Philip, now, in virtue of his wife Joanna, King of Castile, was, very opportunely for the English king and for the Merchant Adventurers, wrecked with his consort upon the shores of England. The business-like King Henry turned the enforced visit to good account, and procured from the Archduke a new agreement so much more favourable to England, that the Flemings termed it the *Intercursus malus*.[1] This agreement, dated the 30th of April 1506, was not ratified owing to Philip's death, more untimely to England than the storm which made him an unwilling guest. Notwithstanding, another agreement, by which the English merchants still profited though not to the same extent as if the *Intercursus malus* had come into force, was provisionally concluded on the 5th of June 1507;[1] and on the 14th of June in that year fresh Letters Patent were issued empowering the Merchant Adventurers to trade freely into Holland, Zeeland, Brabant, and Flanders in accordance with the provision in the 1505 charter, which had contemplated the renewal of friendly relations with these countries. To these Letters Patent reference is made in the Elizabethan charter of 1564. Less than two years after they were granted, in April

The *Intercursus malus* and the Letters Patent of 14 June 1507.

[1] See Pollard (*ut sup.*), vol. ii, pp. 322-4.

1509, Henry VII died, and the Merchant Adventurers lost a king who had the merchants' instinct, and appreciated better than most rulers of England before or since the commercial interests of his people.

The reign of Henry VIII. The Greshams.   Henry VIII renewed the Adventurers' charter, but his reign, so notable in most respects in English history, left little mark upon the record of the fellowship. One name, however, comes into mention during its years, of which much is heard in connexion with the Adventurers a little later—the name of Gresham.   We read that in the year 1533 the governor of the company at Antwerp was William Gresham.[1]   The Greshams were mercers and Merchant Adventurers, and this was the uncle of Sir Thomas Gresham, referred to as 'young Thomas Gresham' in 1543,[1] in which year he was admitted as a member of the Mercers' Company. In April 1520—the year of the Field of the Cloth of Gold—a new commercial convention had been concluded with regard to the trade between England and the Low Countries, in which it was provided that no higher dues should be levied upon English imports than were specified in the treaty with Philip the Good in 1446,[2] but the account sent

---

[1] See *State Papers King Henry VIII*, vol. vii (1849), p. 491, and vol. ix, p. 418; the papers being dated from Antwerp, August 1533, and from Brussels, June 1543.

[2] For this treaty of 11 April 1520, see *Articles offered to the Council by the Merchants Adventurers upon occasion of the treaty with the Dutch*, 3 November 1653 (Rymer), *ut sup.*

home to Thomas Cromwell in 1533 of the state of
the market at Antwerp at that date did not point
to any great expansion of the English cloth trade.
'The merchants of England', writes the correspondent, 'have but easy sale of their clothes,
and not so good as I had thought: it is neither
much to be praised, nor discommended.'[1]

Edward VI again renewed the Adventurers' The reign
charter, and it is in his reign that Sir Thomas of Edward
VI. Sir
Gresham comes to the front in their story. At Thomas
Gresham.
the end of 1551 or beginning of 1552, he became
Royal Agent or King's Merchant at Antwerp, the
confidential financial adviser of the sovereign,
bringing to his duties thorough knowledge of business and a convenient absence of scruple. The
Adventurers were now made to finance the Crown
by means of forced loans, shouldering the debts
which weighted Edward VI and the early years
of Elizabeth.[2] But while Gresham was resolved
that his fellow merchants should contribute to the
royal necessities, he was far from wishing to under-
mine the Adventurers' Fellowship. On the contrary,
as an Adventurer himself, and especially as a
Londoner, he wished to reconstitute it on what
he considered to be a sounder basis. To his mind
the law of 1496 had been a great mistake. The
lowering of the admission fee had brought into the

---

[1] See note 1, p. 74.
[2] For these forced loans see Burgon's *Life and Times of Sir Thomas
Gresham* (1839), vol. i, p. 98, and App. VIII, and pp. 257, &c.

company a number of inexperienced men, with
the result that English traders and their wares
had lost caste, and the course of exchange had set
against England. 'In the few years since this act
was made for the new Hanse, the merchants and our
commodities hath fallen in decay, and like to fall
daily more and more, except the matter be prevented
in time.' So he wrote to the Duke of Northumberland on the 16th of April 1553, urging 'that there
shall be no more made free of this company of the
Merchant Adventurers of the new Hanse from
this day forward'. An attempt was made by
Northumberland to legislate on these lines, but
it came to nothing. It would seem that Gresham
wanted to convert the fellowship again into a more
or less exclusive fellowship of London merchants ;
in this he was unsuccessful; but in a few years'
time his views prevailed in two important respects :
the admission fee to the fellowship was raised, and
the retailer was excluded from its ranks. He contended 'that there may be no retailer occupy the
feat of Merchant Adventurers . . . and likewise the
Merchant Adventurer to occupy his feat only, and
to touch no retail'. This became a cardinal principle of the fellowship, and it was embodied in the
Hamburg Agreement of 1618.[1]

---

[1] For Gresham's letter to the Duke of Northumberland see *Cal. S.P.
Foreign*, 1547-53, p. 264. Extracts from it are printed in Froude's
History of England, chap. xxix (1860 ed., vol. v, pp. 469-73 and
notes), and in Burgon's *Life and Times of Sir Thomas Gresham* (1839),
vol. i, pp. 97 and 463-4, App. VII.

Philip and Mary, like their predecessor, renewed the Adventurers' charter. And then we come to the reign of Queen Elizabeth, which, with that of Henry VII, stands out in strongest relief in the story. In the first year of the reign, 1558-9, an important Act was passed[1]—' an Act for the shipping in English bottoms'—which repealed the Navigation Laws of Richard II and Henry VII, but provided that English subjects who used foreign vessels in time of peace should pay the customs duties to which aliens were liable. An exception was made in favour of ' the merchants commonly called Merchants Adventurers and Merchants of the Staple', with the object of ' the sure and safe conveyance of the wares and merchandises into the parts of Flanders Holland Zeeland or Brabant or any of them'. If no English ships were available, these merchants were allowed to employ foreign vessels without paying the aliens' dues, ' at their several fleets or shippings of cloth and wool, and either of them, from and out of the river of Thames only being made twice in one year at the most'. Here is evidence of the importance of the wool and cloth trade with the Low Countries and of the merchants who handled it, evidence too that the great outlet for the trade from England was the Port of London, and that in London the Merchant Adventurers were stronger than in any other English city. The two sailings a year will be noted, whereas in King

[1] 1 Eliz., cap. 13.

Henry VII's reign the free mart at Calais was held every quarter,[1] and quarterly marts seem to have been the usual practice.

The charter of 1564.

A few years later, on the 18th of July 1564, Queen Elizabeth gave the Adventurers a new charter,[2] which, as supplemented by a later charter from the same queen in 1586, may be taken to have finally defined their status and their constitution. Gresham had forced the Adventurers to find money for the queen at the beginning of her reign : in turn he inspired the new grant which they now received. His name appears in the charter in the list of the first beneficiaries, and another name is that of Thomas Rowe or Roe, Lord Mayor of London in 1568, and grandfather of Sir Thomas Roe, who a little later served England so well in India and at Constantinople. The immediate cause of the charter of 1564 was the foreign complications which are recorded below. As is recited in it, the fellowship's operations in the Low Countries had been for the time suspended, and they had been driven farther afield than Holland, Zeeland, Brabant, and Flanders, the area covered by their previous charter : they had found their way to

---

[1] Burgon (*Life and Times of Sir Thomas Gresham* (*ut sup.*), vol. i, p. 188) says that in the beginning of Elizabeth's reign the Merchant Adventurers sent cloths twice a year, at Christmas and Whitsuntide, into the Low Countries, about 100,000 pieces of cloth annually, valued at £700,000 or £800,000.

[2] This charter is reprinted in Appendix II to *The Early Chartered Companies*, Cawston and Keane (*ut sup.*), pp. 254-77.

East Friesland, Hamburg, and even to Lübeck; and it was doubtful whether the former grants applied. Accordingly the new charter met the case by extending their sphere of trade to East Friesland, West Friesland, and Hamburg, though not to Lübeck, and at the same time it determined the position of the company in far fuller measure than any previous grant. The members were now for the first time constituted a legal corporation with perpetual succession and a common seal, under the title of ' The Governor Assistants and Fellowship of the Merchants Adventurers of England ' ; the national character of the company being proclaimed by the addition of the last words to the existing title of Merchant Adventurers, and being enforced by a provision that any member who married a foreign wife or acquired real property in a foreign country should *ipso facto* lose his membership.[1] There is a reference in the charter to membership by patrimony and apprenticeship, otherwise full authority was given to the Governor Assistants and Fellowship to admit to the company ' all and every such person and persons as they by their discretions shall think meet and convenient and in such manner and form and with such conditions and distinctions and diversity in Freedom as by them shall be thought from time to time

---

[1] The Merchants of the Steelyard had a similar provision, that any one of them who married an English wife should lose his hanse or membership.

most expedient and necessary'. These wide terms
may well have been drafted by Gresham : they
gave discretion to raise the membership fee, to
exclude the retailer, to lay down any rules and
conditions that commended themselves at any given
time to the members of the fellowship and their
governing body. Special interest attaches to the
words 'diversity in freedom', as evidence that
different degrees of membership had come or were
coming into being with corresponding grades of
privileges. The power of electing the governor
and assistants, whose number remained as under
the charter of 1505, was vested in the members
of the fellowship residing beyond the sea, and
beyond the sea it was necessarily contemplated
should be the seat of government, though full power
was given to the governor and his deputies to call
'courts and congregations of all the said Fellowship',
as well at ' the place or places of old time accustomed
within the city of London and elsewhere within
this our realms', as beyond the sea. The governor
and assistants were to make the laws, which were
to be consonant with the laws of England, to have
full jurisdiction in all private causes, and full
authority over English interlopers 'intermeddling
exercising and using the feat or trade of the said
Merchant Adventurers'.

When this charter was granted, the Muscovy or
Russia company had come into being, the Levant
company was soon to be born, a new era of char-

tered companies had dawned, and the Fellowship of
Merchant Adventurers was incorporated on more
modern lines. The general drift of the charter
was to constitute one national company, as far as
possible, of all wholesale English merchants dealing
with the cloth trade to the countries bordering on
the North Sea, to merge London in England, to
make a single fellowship, whose government should
be, even more than in the past, domiciled beyond
the sea, outside the reach of local jealousy and
metropolitan or provincial patriotism, a self-governing body of distinctively English citizens, standard-
ized, regulated, worthily representing and upholding
England and England's great industry in the commercial centres of the neighbouring continent.

The charter of 1564 extended the sphere of the
Merchant Adventurers to Friesland and to Hamburg. By the Eastland Charter of 1579, to which
reference will be made presently,[1] they were given
concurrent rights with the Eastland merchants of
trading in Germany between the Elbe and the
Oder, and also, with exceptions, in Denmark. On
the 28th of April 1586 the Adventurers received
yet another charter from Queen Elizabeth,[2] and in
it Germany is specifically named. They might
trade, into, from and with the country of Germany;
they might hold their meetings 'in the countries
of Germany and the provinces cities and towns

*The East-
land
Charter
of 1579.*

*The
charter of
1586.*

[1] See below, pp. 118, 162-4.
[2] The charter will be found in the 1661 volume, *ut sup.*

thereof'. The charter of 1586 was directed against
interlopers into the Merchant Adventurers' trade—
the standing difficulty of chartered companies.
Former grants were confirmed : fuller powers were
given to deal with interloping traders or with con-
tumacious members of the company ; and English
subjects, not free of the fellowship, were definitely
forbidden to trade with the lands to which the
Merchant Adventurers by their charters were authorized to trade.   One provision in the charter is
of special interest. The terms ran that, inasmuch
as the said Fellowship of Merchant Adventurers of
England or some part of them were often resident
at different places both within the realm and beyond
the seas, 'and to the intent that good government
and rule may be had over every member of the
same fellowship and that the laws and ordinances
to be made as aforesaid may be duly executed in
all places wheresoever any part of the same fellowship shall be resient and abiding,' the members
of the fellowship resident beyond the seas might
choose for every place, whether in England or
beyond the seas, where any part of the fellowship
was to be found, one Deputy and so many associates,
to put into execution the laws of the fellowship
and to settle disputes. The appointment and the
removal of these local officers was entirely vested
in the fellowship beyond the seas, and the provision
itself, with the terminology ' part of the same fellowship ', is conclusive evidence that, as constituted in

the reign of Elizabeth, the Merchant Adventurers of England were one body, not a federation, and that all the local centres, in England or out of it, were entirely subordinate to the governing body beyond the sea. As the years go on, so the charters of these companies, in their earliest stages concerned exclusively with rule and regulation, have a more direct bearing upon trade monopoly ; and, on the other hand, with the mention of monopoly are coupled exceptions framed in modern guise. Thus, while this charter of 1586 contains a definite prohibition against interlopers, there is also a proviso that the buying of horses, harness, powder or other war munitions, books, corn, butter and cheese, flesh and fish, should be free to all English subjects. Notably the free import of corn into England was an object of solicitude, as we shall see in connexion with the Eastland trade.[1]

When this charter of 1586 was granted, England was fighting Spain, and in two years' time came the crowning victory over the Spanish Armada. Before the Spanish troubles began, the Adventurers were at the zenith of their prosperity. Known as 'the English nation beyond the sea', they well merited the title by the volume of their trade and the strength of their organization. As previously at Bruges, and as later at Hamburg, there was at Antwerp an 'English house', an historic house made

The prosperity of the Merchant Adventurers in the middle the sixteenth century.

---

[1] See below, pp. 168, 170.

over to them by the city, to be their central home and meeting place.[1]   In the city of Antwerp it was estimated that some 20,000 people were in the main fed and supported by their trade, some 30,000 more in the rest of the Netherlands.   It was said that Charles V, wishing to introduce the Inquisition into Antwerp, desisted from his purpose on learning that, if it were carried out, the Englishmen would leave both the city and the Low Countries altogether. At a later date, about the end of the century, the total export of English cloth was valued at a million sterling,[2] and the amount and value must have been at least as great before the trade was hampered by political complications.

Troubles in the Low Countries.

With the accession of Philip II to the sovereignty of the Low Countries, and with the regency of Margaret of Parma, English and Protestant merchants in the cities of Flanders and Brabant had troublous times ahead.   In 1563 the Duchess of Parma placed an embargo upon the importation of English cloth, ostensibly because the plague was

---

[1] Wheeler tells us (p. 17) that in 1446 the town of Antwerp confirmed the privileges given to the Merchant Adventurers in that year by Philip the Good, ' giving to them besides a large house, which is now called the old Burse, and afterwards by exchange, another more goodly, spacious, and sumptuous house, called the Court of Lier, which the company enjoyed till the said town was yielded up to the Duke of Parma, in the year 1585 '.   See Burgon (ut sup.), vol. i, p. 72.   He says that the house was the Hôtel Van Lyere, having been the residence of a burgomaster of that name, and was given to the Adventurers on 11 October 1558 (the first year of Queen Elizabeth's reign).

[2] See Wheeler, pp. 20, 24, 25.

rife that year in England,[1] and in the following
year the Adventurers sent their ships to Emden The Ad-
venturers
in East Friesland,[2] and apparently made it their move to
head-quarters for the time being.   They seem, while Emden.
retaining their mart at Emden, to have come back
to Antwerp, where new and more formidable troubles
beset them.   The Duke of Alva had succeeded the
Duchess of Parma as King Philip's Governor-
General in the Netherlands.   In December 1568
Queen Elizabeth intercepted at Plymouth a cargo
of Spanish gold on its way to Flanders.   Alva
retorted by seizing the goods and arresting the
persons of the English merchants at Antwerp and
elsewhere within his reach, and the Queen in turn
arrested Spanish subjects in England.[3]

[1] Wheeler (pp. 51-2) says that the prohibition was ostensibly
because of the plague in England, but really as a reprisal for certain
prohibitions of Flemish goods in England.   Cf. Burgon, vol. ii,
pp. 45-6.

[2] See Stow's *Annals*, 1631 ed., p. 656 : ' Our cloth fleet was sent to
Embden in East Frieseland about Easter next following in Ann:
1564.'

[3] It is again exceedingly difficult to follow the exact movements of
the Adventurers at this time and to ascertain the exact dates and
details.   In Rymer, under the year 1652 (1725 ed., pp. 625-8), will be
found *A chronological deduction concerning the English cloth, out of the
treaties between the House of Burgundy and the Crown of England.*
This document states that by Proclamation of 8 February 1563
various exports to and imports from England were prohibited in the
Spanish Netherlands ; by Proclamation of 22 May 1564 all trade
with the English and all trade into England and Emden was prohibited ; on 30 October 1565 an Act was published interpreting the
Proclamation of 1564 and specifying English kerseys ; on 20 July
1565 all woollen cloth and draperies made in England were banished
out of the Low Countries ; on 15 July 1566 provisional free trade on

Richard
Clough.

When the Adventurers were faced in 1563 with prohibition at Antwerp, they seem to have hesitated for some time as to whether they should send their ships to Emden or to Hamburg. Neither place commended itself to a man who thoroughly knew both the cloth trade and the Merchant Adventurers. This was Richard Clough, of Denbigh, who finds a place in Fuller's *Worthies*, and who was Gresham's factor at Antwerp and a voluminous correspondent. Of Emden he wrote about the beginning of 1564 : ' The people of the town are rude both in word and deed, not meet to entertain merchants.' [1] Notwithstanding, Emden appears to have met the case for the time being, and the people of Emden appreciated the presence of the English merchants among

both sides was re-established ; on 29 May 1574 there was a publication by the great commander of Castile that the English nation should pass the Schelde to Antwerp, the general prohibition notwithstanding. By this date Alva had been recalled and the Dutch insurgents held the mouth of the river. Burgon, ii. 45, &c., makes the date of the Duchess of Parma's prohibition 28 November 1563 ; and states that negotiations took place, and that in November 1564 it was agreed that pending them there should be free intercourse ; that, though Bruges and Antwerp were anxious for the Merchant Adventurers to return, the negotiations broke down in June 1566, though free intercourse was provisionally maintained. At the end of 1568 came the rupture with Alva, and intercourse was renewed in March 1572. In the *History of the Worshipful Company of the Drapers of London*, 1914–15, by the Rev. A. H. Johnson, vol. ii, p. 457, App. XXX A, will be found references to the Deputy and Company of Merchant Adventurers at Hamburg in 1570 ; to the Governor of Merchant Adventurers in Antwerp in 1574 ; to the Governor and Assistants of the Merchant Adventurers at Bruges in 1576.

[1] See Burgon, ii. 59. For Clough see Burgon, i. 235-41, &c., and *Dict. Nat. Biog.*, s.v.

them, as did all the cities wherein the Merchant
Adventurers sojourned.

The mention of Hamburg in the charter of 1564 The
of itself proves that at this time the company had beginning
either already secured a footing in this Hanseatic Hamburg
city or were on the point of securing it. On the con-
19th of July 1567 the English merchants made nexion.
a ten years' contract with the senate of Hamburg
for permission to trade and reside in the city: some
trial ships were sent there in 1568, and at the end
of May 1569 the cloth fleet arrived in the Elbe,
bringing with it Richard Clough, who had apparently been appointed deputy for the company
at Hamburg: he died there in the following year.
The Adventurers now went into residence at Hamburg, where, as at Antwerp, they were given at the
public expense an 'English House'; but their first
stay in the city was brief: the contract was abrogated
or came to an end in 1578.[1]

[1] See Wheeler, pp. 138-9. See also *A Discourse concerning Freedom
of Trade*, by Henry Parker, 1648, p. 24. This pamphlet is very valuable,
as it is written from Hamburg. See also *Hamburgh Complaints*,
H. of C. Paper 181, 20 April 1835, p. 9. Archdeacon Cunningham
(*The Growth of English Trade Industry and Commerce in Modern Times*,
Pt. I, 1907, pp. 226-7) says, following Ehrenburg, that the Senate of
Hamburg first invited the Merchant Adventurers to the city in 1564.
A good account of the beginning of the Merchant Adventurers' connexion with Hamburg is given by Burgon, vol. ii, pp. 316-31. The
year 1578, in which the contract came to an end, was the year in
which Queen Elizabeth cancelled the special privileges of the Hanse
Merchants in London, and Macpherson (*ut sup.*), vol. ii, p. 161, says
that she took this step because the Hansards shut out the English
merchants from Hamburg. According to the *Hamburgh Complaints*,
Blue Book, p. 9, 'The Senate of Hamburgh, in the year 1567, and

Commercial intercourse with the Low Countries had meanwhile been intermittently renewed; but in 1585 England was at open war with Spain, and in that year Antwerp, 'the late packhouse of Europe',[1] to whose greatness, surpassing that of all other trade centres of the time, the Merchant Adventurers had notably contributed,[2] capitulated to the Prince of Parma and his army. Excluded from Brabant and Flanders, and no longer welcomed at Hamburg, the Adventurers gravitated back to Emden,[3] whence they moved to Stade on the Elbe, lower down the river than Hamburg. Here they traded for some ten years, bringing

The Adventurers at Stade.

afterwards by the contract of 1618, granted to the English merchants, to enable them to assemble for the regulation of their affairs, extensive premises in the centre of the town, afterwards called " The English House ".' The contract of 1618, which is given on pp. 17-24 of the Blue Book, states in article 18, ' And for the sake of establishing a good order of things, we have given to the said company a certain place and a privileged house, which we will keep in repair, to use and enjoy with citizen's rights, and where they may freely, securely, and without hindrance assemble as often as they please, &c.'. Cf. Burgon, vol. ii, p. 331, and Dr. Lingelbach, ' The Merchant Adventurers at Hamburg,' American Historical Review, vol. ix, 1903-4. Dr. Lingelbach says that the Hamburg Senate bought ' the English House' and handed it over to the Adventurers in 1570.

[1] Wheeler, p. 19.

[2] 'In the space of 60 or 70 years, whereas it had, before it was our mart, not above 4 able merchants and six ships, it became the glorious magazine of all Europe,' Parker, A Discourse concerning Freedom of Trade (ut sup.), p. 12.

[3] ' From Hamburg we removed to Embden,' Parker (p. 24). ' From Embden we betook ourselves to Stade, and there we continued till 1597 ' (p. 25). They seem to have gone to Stade in 1587. The English government appears not to have given them adequate support in their trade at Emden. See Burgon, vol. ii, pp. 316-18.

riches and abnormal prosperity to a small German town within easy distance of Hamburg, even as the Eastlanders planted themselves at Elbing near unto Dantzic. But at Stade they found no sure resting-place.[1]

As the Merchant Adventurers were on the Continent, so were the Hanse merchants in England, and had been for centuries, a powerful, privileged, self-governing colony of alien merchants. Known as the Easterlings, or the merchants of Almayne, down to the time of Edward VI they maintained their status under the aegis of successive kings of England, who had their *quid pro quo* in money lent; and by the Treaty of Utrecht, in 1474, Edward IV had confirmed to them in perpetuity the Steelyard, which adjoined their official building, the *Guildhalla Teutonicorum*, in Dowgate Ward by the side of the Thames. Hansards and Merchant Adventurers alike contended for special rights in other lands than their own: the one and the other bitterly attacked their rivals for following the same courses which they pursued themselves. When Henry VII broke off relations with the Flemings, and for the time the Merchant Adventurers were deprived of the

The Hansards in London.

[1] Dr. Lingelbach (' *The Merchant Adventurers at Hamburg,*' *American Historical Review*, vol. ix, 1903-4, p. 269 note) says that, while the Adventurers were at Stade, the chief mart and residence of the fellowship was still in the Netherlands, having been established at Middelburg in 1587, i.e. after the agreement with the States General of 9 January 1587; but it is difficult to harmonize this with the Adventurers' own statement that their settled mart in the Netherlands dated from 1596, referred to below, p. 92.

Flemish markets, the Hansards, privileged neutrals as they were, profited thereby, and this was gall and bitterness to the Merchant Adventurers. The outcome in 1493 was a serious riot in London, and an attempt to storm the Steelyard.[1] The riot was quelled, the German merchants were not ousted, and under Henry VIII, who, it was said, wanted their money for his foreign wars, their privileges were confirmed. But the Merchant Adventurers grew stronger as the years went on, and towards the end of Edward VI's reign, in 1552,[2] they prevailed upon the king's council to cancel the special rights which the Germans had so long enjoyed, one reason given being that the Hansards, not content with dealing with their own lands and cities, carried English merchandise to the Low Countries—the special preserve of the Merchant Adventurers. There is a statement, which must have been exaggerated, that 'It was proved that the Stillyard men in the year 1551 shipped 44000 cloths, and all the English merchants together did not export above 1100'.[3] Queen Mary in 1554

[1] See Holinshed's *Chronicles*, 1808 ed., vol. iii, p. 508. For the Hansards in London see Strype's edition of Stow's *Survey*, vol. i, Bk. II, pp. 202–5.

[2] Strype (*ut sup.*, Bk. II, p. 205) makes the date 1551, and Edward VI's decision the last word on the subject. 'In the year 1551 the fifth of Edward VI, through complaints of the English merchants, the liberty of the Steelyard merchants was siezed into the king's hands, and so it resteth.'

[3] From Rapin's *History of England*, 2nd ed., 1733, vol. ii, Bk. XVI, pp. 24–5.

restored the old privileges for three years, but subsequently cancelled them again ; and Elizabeth, after characteristic waiting on events, in 1578 took the same course. The Merchant Adventurers had won the victory. But they suffered for it. In revenge the Hansards prevailed upon the German Emperor Rudolf to issue a decree on the 1st of August 1597, which prohibited the English merchants from trafficking in Germany, on the ground, so Camden tells us, that 'they practised their trade and sold their wares there by the laws of England, and not those of the Empire'.[1] Queen Elizabeth retorted by expelling the Hansards in the following year from her dominions and handing over the Steelyard to the Lord Mayor of London.[2]

Merchant Adventurers driven from Germany.

There was now no refuge for the Merchant Adventurers, save in the Seven United Provinces. They had been made free to trade there by a grant of the States General of the 9th of January 1587, supplemented by another notification of the 14th of July 1598.[3] In a petition addressed to Cromwell

The Adventurers in the United Netherlands.

[1] Camden's *History of Queen Elizabeth.* See *A Complete History of England*, 1706, vol. ii, p. 600. The Emperor's decree, as given in Wheeler, alleged that 'the foresaide Adventurers' colleges were heretofore forbidden and banished out of Dantsick in Prussia' (Wheeler, p. 117). Probably this is a confusion between the Merchant Adventurers and the Eastlanders.

[2] An Imperial edict against the Merchant Adventurers had been launched in 1582, but on the remonstrance of the Emden authorities it was not put into force (Parker, *A Discourse concerning Freedom of Trade*, p. 25).

[3] See *Articles offered to the Council by the Merchant Adventurers*

in 1656 they asserted that they had had a settled mart in the Netherlands since 1596.[1] They were invited to Groningen, but at first made their headquarters at Middelburg in Zeeland, where in 1601 Wheeler's account and defence of the company was printed by the printer to the States of Zeeland.

The Adventurers, however, had proved themselves abundantly to be a valuable asset to the towns in which they made their marts: they brought trade and riches wherever they went, and the profit which followed in the wake of English enterprise was, except in moments of irritation, a stronger attraction than trade rivalry coupled with race prejudice. Emden and Stade made it clear that they would welcome the Englishmen's return,[2] and very soon Hamburg followed suit. In 1603–4 negotiations took place at Bremen between the English government and the Hanse cities, in 1611 an agreement was arrived at between the Senate of Hamburg and the Merchant Adventurers, and this agreement was The contract with Hamburg of 1618. explained and extended by a formal contract concluded on the 2nd of June 1618,[3] under which the position of the Adventurers at Hamburg was assured in the fullest manner and with the most ample

upon occasion of the treaty with the Dutch, 3 November 1653 (Rymer), *ut sup.*

[1] *Cal. of S. P. Dom.*, 1655–6, pp. 334–5.

[2] See Rymer, 8 October 1597 (for Emden); 3 February 1601 (for Stade).

[3] See *Hamburgh Complaints*, H. of C. Paper 181, 20 April 1835, p. 11, and for the contract itself, pp. 17–24.

privileges. The Hansards in turn were reinstated in possession of the Steelyard, though they were never replaced upon the specially privileged basis in the city of London which in old times they had enjoyed. Among the many rights conferred upon the Englishmen at Hamburg in the many articles of the contract of 1618, it need hardly be said that freedom of religious worship found a place.

In or about this same year, 1618, John Milton's father engaged as tutor for his son, Thomas Young, the son of a Scotch Presbyterian minister, and in 1622 Young went out to Hamburg as chaplain to the English merchants, remaining there for some six years, and at a later date becoming Master of Jesus College, Cambridge.[1] *Thomas Young.*

From 1618 onwards the Adventurers' operations were divided between the Netherlands and Hamburg. In the Netherlands their head-quarters were at first at Middelburg, as already told. In 1621 they moved to Delft. About fifteen or sixteen years later they moved to Rotterdam, and after the Dutch War of 1652–4 they found their final home in the Netherlands at Dordrecht or Dort. During the greater part of their stay at Delft, between 1623 and 1633, their deputy there was Edward Misselden, merchant and economist, author of *Free Trade and the Means to make Trade flourish* and of *The Circle of Commerce*, a vigorous controversialist, upholding the case of the Merchant Adventurers *The marts in the Netherlands.* *Edward Misselden.*

---

[1] For Thomas Young see *Dict. Nat. Biog.*, s.v.

as against the Staplers, whose champion, equally voluble in controversy, was Gerald Malynes. Unlike the Puritan Thomas Young, Misselden was in harmony with the views of Archbishop Laud, which were not, it would seem, the views of the majority of Merchant Adventurers.[1] While the Adventurers were domiciled at Middelburg, at Middelburg was the main seat of government for the fellowship. At a later date, in the middle of the century if not before, Hamburg became the head centre, and remained so to the end: in the earlier years the principal residence and mart of the company, in the latest stages its one and only home beyond the seas.[2]

King James I cancels the Adventurers' charter and again renews it.
Meanwhile the Adventurers had weathered a crisis in England. King James I began his reign by renewing their charter on the 25th of May 1604, but within ten years there was trouble between the company and the king. The company had the monopoly of the cloth trade with the Netherlands, and was licensed to export cloth, undyed and un-

---

[1] For Edward Misselden see *Dict. Nat. Biog.*, s.v.

[2] The date at which Hamburg became the seat of government for the fellowship is usually given as 1650 or 1651. Dr. Lingelbach (*American Historical Review, ut sup.*, p. 274 note) says that he has been unable to ascertain the exact date when Hamburg became the chief centre, but thinks it altogether probable that it became so when the Adventurers shifted their Netherlands residence from Middelburg to the smaller town of Delft in 1621. This, however, can hardly have been the case, for, when corresponding in connexion with the Newcastle controversy, the governing body in 1637 were evidently domiciled in the Netherlands. (See below, p. 137.)

dressed, any statute to the contrary notwithstanding. 'White' cloths, the undyed and undressed articles, formed the staple of their trade, and the dyeing and dressing took place in the Netherlands. That the processes connected with the cloth trade should be carried out in England and not be shared with foreign parts was a not unnatural aspiration of trade selfishness under the cloke of patriotism, and arguments in favour of stimulating the dyeing industry at home and raising a customs revenue on the ingredients which would be imported for the dyers' use, became familiar. But according to the author of *The Request and Suite of a True-hearted Englishman*, which was written in 1553,[1] the English dyers themselves had been to blame. 'The dyers of England', he wrote, 'have raised a foul slander upon the famous river of Thames, and all other waters of this your Majesty's realm'; his allegation being that, to excuse their own ignorance and incompetence, the dyers laid the blame upon English waters as being inferior for dyeing purposes to the waters of the Low Countries. His

William Cholmeley's pamphlet.

---

[1] This pamphlet is printed in *The Camden Miscellany*, 1853: for the quotations see pp. 3, 5, 7, 13, 19. Reference is made to it in Froude's *History of England*, chap. xxvii, 1860 ed., vol. v, p. 280. The contention that foreigners could not get on without English wool or cloth was a very old one. See the poem of Edward IV's reign on England's Commercial Policy :

'For there is no reme [realm] in no manner degree,
But they have need to our English commodity.'

Political Poems and Songs from Edward III to Richard III, edited by Thomas Wright, 1859, vol. ii, pp. 282, &c.

defence of the Thames is an echo of the words of
Naaman the Syrian, 'Are not Abana and Pharpar,
rivers of Damascus, better than all the waters of
Israel?' He was William Cholmeley, a Londoner
and a grocer, of limited means, and he had put the
matter to the test. He had brought over an expert
dyer from Antwerp, and taking into partnership
a dyer in Southwark, had for three years made his
venture pay; he then proceeded to wake up his
countrymen. He pointed out that 'yearly there is
carried out of this realm by English merchants and
strangers to the number of 150,000 broad cloths at
the least, undyed and undressed', and 'that the
same be all wrought in Flanders, Holland, Brabant,
Zeeland, Eastland, and Dutchland, to the setting at
work of two hundred thousand persons and above'.
He contended that all the work should be done in
England, and the mart should be in England, for
where the cloth is merchants must come: so would
London take from Antwerp the immense trade
which was concentrated at the great city on the
Schelde. Setting up the objections which were or
might be raised to his proposals, he proceeded to
knock them down. One objection was, 'If we
should not have our mart beyond the seas and let
them have our cloth undressed and undyed, they
would make cloth themselves; so should we be in
a far worse taking than now, for then we should
have no utterance of our cloth at all'. To this his
answer was, 'I grant they will make cloth, and

they do make cloth, yes even as good as any is made in England, but not without English wool'. He urged accordingly that workmen should be brought over to teach the English handicraftsmen the secrets of dyeing, that the Lord Mayor and Aldermen should be charged 'to see that in the City of London all manner of cloth be truly and perfectly dyed, after the manner of Antwerp', and that no cloth dyed beyond the seas should be sold in London.

Notwithstanding William Cholmeley and his cogent arguments, the cloth trade kept on its course, and the Merchant Adventurers exported the unfinished articles. It was a working compromise, by which England and the Low Countries shared the profits of the trade. In King James's reign the discontent of those who thought on Cholmeley's lines came to a head: the English dyers and clothworkers raised a protest against the refusal of the Merchant Adventurers to export dyed and dressed goods: the king and his council took the matter into consideration and supported the protest: the Adventurers refused to comply, inasmuch as such goods commanded no sale upon the Continent: the outcome was a Royal Proclamation of 22 July 1614 prohibiting the export of cloths, undyed and undressed, after the following 2nd of November; and a further Proclamation upon the 2nd of December in the same year 'prohibiting the Merchant Adventurers' charter from henceforth to be put in practise or execution either within the kingdom or beyond the seas'.[1]

Cokayne's company.
On the 29th of August 1615 a charter was given to a new company, formed to carry out the king's behest, and entitled 'The Governor Assistants and Fellowship of the King's Merchants Adventurers of the new Trade of London'.[2] The prime mover in the venture, and the governor of the new company, was William Cokayne, a great friend of King James. His father had been governor of the Eastland Company, he himself was a Merchant Adventurer, an Alderman of the City of London, and shortly afterwards—in 1619–20—Lord Mayor.[3] But most of the members of the new company had not his standing and experience. 'The company', wrote Bacon on the 14th of October 1616, 'consists of a number of young men and shopkeepers, which not being bred in the trade, are fearful to meddle with any of the dear and fine cloths'[4]—words which recall Sir Thomas Gresham's criticism of the 'New Hanse' in the Merchant Adventurers' fellowship, who had been called into existence by the lowering of the membership fee. But, if they had been the most experienced men in the world, they would

[1] The Proclamation is printed at pp. 296-9 of *The Early Chartered Companies*, Cawston and Keane, *ut sup.*

[2] This charter will be found printed in Carr, *Select Charters of Trading Companies, ut sup.*, pp. 78–98.

[3] For Sir William Cokayne see *Dict. Nat. Biog.*, s.v. No mention, however, is there made of this episode.

[4] See *Letters and Life of Francis Bacon*, by James Spedding, vol. vi (1872), p. 83.

have failed. Even before the charter was granted, Cokayne and his associates found themselves wholly unable to carry out the policy in furtherance of which they had supplanted the old company. The objection which William Cholmeley thought he had answered, materialized and proved insurmountable. The result of prohibiting the export of undyed and undressed cloth was not, as had been contemplated, that the Dutch were compelled to buy the dyed and dressed cloth from England, but that they set up looms throughout the Netherlands in order to dispense with English cloth altogether, whether or not they drew their supplies of wool from England. Concessions were made to the new company, allowing them to export a certain amount of undressed cloth, but without avail: the complaints lately directed against the Merchant Adventurers were now directed against themselves, as the English clothworkers felt the want of trade: Gloucestershire, Worcestershire, Wiltshire, protested: 'the subjects of this kingdom generally', wrote Bacon, 'have an ill taste and conceit of the new company.'[1] In a word, they had a brief and most inglorious existence, and on the 12th of August 1617 appeared another Royal Proclamation 'for restoring the Ancient Merchants Adventurers to their former trade and privileges'.[2] The episode

[1] *Letters and Life of Francis Bacon, ut sup.*, vol. vi, p. 84, under date 14 October 1616.

[2] For this Proclamation see Cawston and Keane (*ut sup.*), pp. 300–3.

is of special interest in that Francis Bacon advised
the government in the difficulties in which they
found themselves involved, and the occasion called
forth the following memorable saying of the great
man : 'I do confess I did ever think that trading
in companies is most agreeable to the English
nature, which wanteth that same general vein of
a Republic which runneth in the Dutch and serveth
to them instead of a company.'[1]

The charter of 1618. That King James had delivered himself into the
hands of the Merchants Adventurers is very evident
from the terms of the new charter, which they
secured on the 28th of January 1618, having, it
would seem, bought off the opposition of Thomas
Howard, Earl of Suffolk, Lord Treasurer of England,
by a bribe of £3,000.[2] The charter makes a
plaintive reference to the good intentions which
had inspired the abortive Cokayne scheme, 'to
establish and scale the dyeing and dressing of
woollen clothes within this realm as a work
specially tending to the employment and maintenance of a great number of our poor subjects';

[1] Bacon, *ut sup.*, vol. v (1869), p. 259, under date 25 February 1616.
For the whole episode see Bacon's *Life and Letters*, vols. v and vi, and
Gardiner's *History of England*, 1603–42, 1883 ed., vol. ii, chap. xxi,
pp. 385–90. See also Motley's *United Netherlands*, chap. 1, 1867 ed.,
vol. iv, pp. 433–4. It will be seen that Motley traces the trouble to
dyers and clothiers who had emigrated from the United Netherlands
to England. As to the effect of King James's action in stimulating
Dutch competition, see below, pp. 170–3.

[2] See the charges against the Earl of Suffolk in 1619, *Letters and
Life of Francis Bacon* (*ut sup.*), vol. vii (1874), p. 57.

and then it proceeds to rivet the monopoly of the resuscitated Merchant Adventurers in the most wholesale fashion. 'To the end that the secret practice of Interlopers and others not free of the said Fellowship of Merchants Adventurers of England may be the better discovered' and the interlopers restrained and suppressed, the Adventurers were authorized to appoint officers to be present in all the custom houses at the various ports of England; to these officers all exporters of woollen goods were to give true entries of the commodities of this nature which they were exporting; the masters of the ships were to give bond that the goods would be carried to the places specified; the Adventurers were to have the right of search on all ships, power to seize woollen goods being exported contrary to the charter, to imprison and fine the offending parties; the custom house officials were not to allow the export of any woollen goods, unless they had been entered with the Adventurers, and not to accept any warrant for export of woollen manufactures unless signed by the Adventurers' officers: in a word, the whole machinery of the government was to be at the disposal of the fellowship for the protection of their monopoly. For the rest, the Adventurers were given full power to levy reasonable taxes upon the commodities in which their members dealt, to hold their meetings in England or beyond the seas, to deal freely with any prince, city, or state as to obtaining and using all manner of rights, jurisdictions, and liberties, and to choose their places of residence in Germany and the Low Countries, mention being also made of the town of Calais. A comparison of this grant with the original charter of 1407 will show how the face of charters had altered in the two centuries which had elapsed. The early charter was solely concerned with rule, with the maintenance of law and order among the merchants to whom it applied: the charter of 1618 was mainly concerned with safeguarding in the most detailed manner a rigid trade monopoly. It was a great triumph for the Adventurers, and, inasmuch as by the contract of 1618 they secured their position at Hamburg, they were now within their own field stronger than ever. Their strength and their vitality, as shown at once by their relations with king and parliament through the troubled middle years of the seventeenth century, and by the bitterness with which they were attacked, is more noteworthy when it is remembered that by this time they were only one among various great English companies, including the East India Company; that English commercial enterprise had widened out into all the world, while they themselves were rather contracting than expanding the area of their operations; that joint stock had come into play in other companies, though not in their own. No longer were they, as they had been at once in fact and in name, 'the English nation beyond the sea': the sea no longer connoted the Narrow Sea, the English

The strength of the Merchant Adventurers.

Channel : from King James's time onward they
were faced on the Continent in a growing degree
with Dutch opposition ; yet they held their own in
a wonderful manner.

The result of the restoration of their charter was *Their*
and could only have been to intensify their mono- *monopoly*
poly of the English cloth trade with the Netherlands *about*
1622.
and Germany. As they were strong, they should
have been merciful, if they had known the things
that belonged to their peace. The charter of 1618
was a triumph, but an impolitic triumph. 'All the
trade of the merchants of the staple, of the merchant
strangers, and of all other English merchants, concerning the exportation of all the commodities made
of wool into those countries where the same are
specially to be vented, is in the power of the
Merchant Adventurers only ; and it is come to be
managed by 40 or 50 persons of that company,
consisting of three or four thousand.'[1] So wrote
Gerard Malynes in 1622, probably underrating the
number of the Adventurers, who in 1648 were
estimated at over 6,000.[2] He wrote as an ardent
champion of the Staplers, a bitter opponent of
the Merchant Adventurers. Staplers and Hansards
alike had gone down before the Adventurers ; home

---

[1] *The Maintenance of Free Trade*, &c., by Gerard Malynes, 1622,
pp. 50–1.

[2] *A Discourse concerning Freedom of Trade*, by Henry Parker, 1648
(*ut sup.*), p. 22. He says that there were at that date 'above 6,000
persons free of our company'. In 1601 Wheeler wrote, 'they are not
so few as 3,500 ' (p. 78).

rivals on the one side, foreign competitors on the other, had found them too strong.

The Inter-
lopers.
But the charter of 1618, with its stringent and irritating restraints on the cloth trade, bore inevitable fruit. Through the century we find a series of complaints from the 'Interlopers', as the members of the company styled the merchants who were not of their number ; free traders, as the interloping merchants would have styled themselves. The Adventurers took for their text the advantage to the kingdom of a regulated and well-ordered traffic through clearly defined channels, as opposed to disorderly and promiscuous dealing. The Interlopers harped upon the evils of restriction and monopoly, though in the latter days of the century, when opposition was directed against the East India Company, proposals were made for a regulated in lieu of joint-stock trade to the East Indies, on the ground that by establishing a regulated trade, which was from first to last the basis of the Merchants Adventurers company, 'the mischief as well as the wrong of a monopoly will be prevented'.[1]

Their
position
in the
seven-
teenth
century.
The 'Interlopers'' influence may be traced in resolutions of the House of Commons markedly hostile to the company, which were passed in 1624.[2]

---

[1] From an undated print, entitled *Proposals for a more beneficial and equal establishment of a regulated company to carry on the Trade to the East Indies,* evidently of the end of the seventeenth century. B.M. 816 m. $\frac{11}{60}$.

[2] 30 April 1624 (H. of C. Journals, vol. i, p. 695). The resolutions were worded : 'That the opinion of this House is that the Impost

Through the century the opponents of the Adventurers, notably the clothiers and merchants of Exeter and the West Country, were vigorous in attacking them;[1] yet on the 7th of December 1634, and again on the 5th of May 1639,[2] the fellowship secured Proclamations from Charles I that cloth and woollen commodities should be exported only to the marts and staple towns of the Adventurers in Germany and in the Netherlands. Wise in their generation, when king and parliament parted company, they sided with parliament as against the king. In the Journals of the House of Commons, in February 1643,[3] there is an entry to the effect

money, set by the Merchant Adventurers upon cloth, is unlawful, unjust, and a grievance to the People; and to be taken off, and no longer to be continued by them '; and, ' That this House thinketh fit that the Merchant Adventurers, and all other merchants, may promiscuously transport to all places all northern and western dosens, kerseys, and new manufactures'. See also pp. 698–9 and 706 for notes of succeeding debates. On p. 706 it will be seen that on 19 May 1624 the House declared ' the Patent of the Merchant Adventurers, as now it is, a grievance both in the creation and execution '.

[1] Macpherson (*ut sup.*), vol. ii, pp. 499, &c., says that the Exeter and West Country merchants and clothiers protested in 1638, 1643, 1645. Another protest came in February 1662. The pamphlet of 1645, *A Discourse consisting of Motives for the Enlargement and Freedom of Trade, &c.*, which has been quoted above, p. 12, is an attack on the Merchant Adventurers. Later in the century (about 1670) is a similar pamphlet, *The Reasons humbly offered to consideration, why the Incorporating the whole trade of the Woollen Manufactures of this Kingdom to the Company called the Merchant Adventurers of England, is and will prove more and more detrimental as to the country in general, so especially to the county of Devon and city of Exon, &c.* (B.M. 712 g. $\frac{16}{8}$).

[2] These proclamations will be found in Rymer.

[3] Vol. ii, p. 982. The date was 27 February 1642–3.

that the king had asked them for a loan of £20,000 : the House of Commons requested them not to lend the money, and thanked them for informing the House of the matter. In that same year the Adventurers lent to parliament a sum of £30,000, at good interest, 8 per cent., and for a good purpose, the use of the navy. They had their reward. In the autumn of the year the Lords and Commons passed an ordinance which confirmed their rights in the fullest manner.[1] The Journals of the House about this date are replete with entries showing the extent to which they financed parliament, and the result seems to have been a load of liabilities [2] which hampered their future. The long life of the great chartered companies and the influence which they exercised upon English history could not be better illustrated than by the case of the Merchant

---

[1] The text of the ordinance will be found in Rymer, 1725 ed., vol. xx, p. 547. It is entitled 'An ordinance of the Lords and Commons in Parliament assembled for upholding the government of the Fellowship of Merchants Adventurers of England, to the better maintenance of the Trade of Clothing and Woollen Manufacture of the Kingdom'. It provided ' That the said fellowship shall continue and be a corporation, and shall have power to levy monies on the members of their corporation, and their goods, for their necessary charge and maintenance of their government, and that no person shall trade into those ports limited by their Incorporation, but such as are free of that Corporation, upon forfeiture of their goods'. Then the fees are prescribed. The H. of C. Journals make this ordinance with the Lords amendments agreed to on 11 October 1643 (vol. iii, p. 273).

[2] Macpherson (vol. ii, p. 502) quotes or summarizes them as saying, in 1661, ' It is true they owe a large debt, occasioned partly by the misfortunes of the civil wars, &c., and partly by the opposition of the Interlopers '.

Adventurers. At the end of the fifteenth century
they had been the mainstay of King Henry VII in
his stand against the Flemings. They found money
for Queen Elizabeth in the straitened early years
of her reign. In the middle of the seventeenth
century they were a powerful factor on the side of
the Commons against the king.

In May 1656 Cromwell,[1] a staunch supporter of Crom-
British trading interests, issued a proclamation up- well's
holding the company and their trade monopoly, with mation.
special reference to their mart in the Netherlands ;
and after the Restoration, Charles II gave them
a new charter confirming their rights. This seems The
to have been the last charter which they received, charter of
and it simply confirmed previous grants, with the
exception of a provision, made in favour of the
liberties and customs of London, that no one living
in London or within twenty miles radius should be
admitted as a Merchant Adventurer, unless he were
free of the City of London.[2]

But the Adventurers' fortunes were now on the The
wane.   In 1662 their West Country opponents the Ad-
renewed their complaints against them, and in May venturers.

---

[1] Dr. Lingelbach (in *The Internal Organization of the Merchant
Adventurers of England*, November, 1901, *Transactions of the Royal
Historical Society*, xvi, 1902, p. 40) points out that the leaders of the
Merchant Adventurers wanted Cromwell to become king.

[2] This is the charter which recites or mentions the older charters in
S. P. Dom. Charles II, 1661, January, vol. xxvii. The Hamburg-
London Agreement of October 22, 1688, given in part at the end of
B. M. Add. MSS. 18913, states that the charter was about to be
renewed ; but, as the cloth trade was thrown open, the renewal prob-
ably did not take place.

of that year the export of all woollen manufactures was thrown open to any place except the company's own two marts at Dort and Hamburg until the following Christmas. This Proclamation was formally revoked in April 1663, as having been ineffectual, and the company was again granted the sole licence to export woollen goods to Germany and the Netherlands,[1] but the renewal of the monopoly was coupled with a drastic reduction of the membership fee. In a statement of their case presented in the last years of the century, the Adventurers traced the decline of their prosperity to the fact, as they alleged, that in Charles II's reign foreigners had been allowed to intermeddle in their trade, especially with the Netherlands.[2] The Dutch Wars must have told sorely against them. Not only did they close for the time entirely one of the two fields of trade, but the English ships plying to and from Hamburg past the coasts of the Netherlands were in constant danger from the powerful Dutch navy. 'Then to

[1] The entry in *Cal. of S. P. Dom.* under date 8 April 1663 (vol. l, 1663-4, p. 103) is interesting, the licence being to export woollen goods to Germany, the United Provinces, Calais, &c. As in the charter of 1618, Calais comes on the scene again, though it had long passed out of English hands.

[2] See *Reasons for Supporting the Company of Merchant Adventurers of England in their Trade to Germany,* an undated print but of the time of William III, after Queen Mary's death in 1694 (B.M. 816 m. $\frac{11}{33}$). The print contains the words, ' It is not proposed but that the trade from Exeter, and all other parts of England, to Holland and Flanders, may be left open and free, as it hath been for several years past'. The mention of Exeter shows the quarter from which the main opposition to the Merchant Adventurers came.

III OF ENGLAND 109

the Change, where great the noise and trouble of having our Hambrough ships lost.'[1] This is an entry in Pepys's diary on the 31st of May 1665, the Adventurers' ships having run, it would seem, into the Dutch fleet by mistake for their own. Strenuous sea-fighters and privateers in war time, in peace the keenest and most unscrupulous trade rivals, the Dutchmen must have had much to say to the decline of the Merchant Adventurers. A little later, at the beginning of the reign of William and Mary, the English cloth trade was thrown open, and the fellowship entered on the eighteenth century with no such monopoly as they had once enjoyed.

The cloth trade thrown open.

When King James I came to the throne of England and peace was made with Spain in 1604, restoring the old privileges which English merchants had in past times enjoyed in the Low Countries,[2] there had been a prospect of the Merchant Adventurers returning to the Spanish Netherlands on the status which they had held half a century before; but, according to their own account, papist English merchants, resident at Antwerp, 'certain Jesuited English merchants and priests together', worked against their fellow countrymen's interests and in their own.[3] Later, in 1649, the Adventurers were

Proposals for returning to Flanders.

[1] *Pepys's Diary*, edited by Henry B. Wheatley, 1894, vol. iv, p. 421 and note.

[2] This treaty of 18 August 1604 between England, Spain, and the Archdukes is given in Stow's *Annals* (1651 ed., pp. 846–55). By Article XX the old privileges were renewed.

[3] *A Chronological Deduction concerning the English Cloth, &c.* (*ut sup.*), Rymer, 1652 (1725 ed., vol. xx, pp. 625–8).

invited to go back to Bruges, and the invitation was renewed in 1651. The invitation was attractive not only because Bruges was their old home, but also because the outbreak of the Dutch War in 1652 for the time being cut off their foothold in the United Netherlands. Accordingly, in November 1652, the Council of State received ' a Petition of the Merchants Adventurers concerning the removing their company from Rotterdam to Flanders '.[1] They asked that three conditions, indispensable to their return, might be laid before the Spanish government: the first was free exercise of the Reformed religion, the petitioners being content that such free exercise should be only 'within the public house of the nation, admitting only English'; the second was security for person and estate, past events in Antwerp making an assurance on this head necessary ; the third was repeal of all Acts and Proclamations ' by which the drapery of this land stands banished ', and the extinction of all payments by way of licence. The argument was used that through the Spanish Netherlands the cloth trade could be carried on into Germany, the trade through the Sound being disturbed by the action of Denmark. Nothing seems to have come of this petition. Protestant merchants were no doubt at a discount under Spanish rule : Flanders knew them no more ; and, when the Dutch War ended in April 1654, they confined

---

[1] This petition is given in Rymer (1725 ed., vol. xx, pp. 623-5), received and considered by the Council of State 4 November 1652.

themselves to their two marts, one in the Netherlands and the other at Hamburg.

One of the grounds of the numerous complaints
against them was that they tied the export of
woollen goods for the Netherlands and Germany
to a single mart in either case. There was a reason
for it : it made the task of regulating the trade more
easy by concentrating it at 'a staple established
under the wholesome government of traffic in the
due order and policy of a fellowship' ;[1] but it did
not commend itself to the Interlopers. The pamphlet of 1645, which has already been quoted, com-
plained that 'the company tieth their numbers to
trade to two towns only, viz. Hamburg and Rotterdam' ;[2] and the West Country protest of 1670 made
the same accusation, 'The company strictly ties
their members to two towns, Hamburg and Dort'.[3]
It is clear from the petition to the Council of State
in 1652 that their head-quarters in the Netherlands
at the outbreak of the Dutch War in that year were
at Rotterdam. When peace came again in 1654,
and trade relations were resumed, they failed to
re-establish themselves at Rotterdam, and came to
terms with the citizens of Dort, planting their mart

The two
marts of
the com-
pany.

[1] These words occur in the petition to the Council of State in 1652
referred to above.

[2] *A Discourse consisting of Motives for the Enlargement and Freedom
of Trade, especially that of Cloth, &c.*, p. 36. See above, pp. 12, 105.

[3] *The Reasons humbly offered to consideration, why the Incorporating the
whole trade of the Woollen Manufactures of this Kingdom to the Company
called the Merchant Adventurers of England, &c.*, p. 6. See above,
p. 105 note.

there in 1655.[1]   The terms were approved in
Cromwell's Proclamation of 1656.   All the Merchant
Adventurers living elsewhere in the Netherlands
at that date were ordered to move to Dort, and the
export of woollen manufactures from England to
the Netherlands was confined to that city.   In spite
of interruption caused by the Dutch Wars of
Charles II's reign, the mart at Dort lasted on till
1751,[2] but after that date the Adventurers left the
Netherlands altogether and confined themselves
wholly to Hamburg.

Fees for member-ship of the com-pany.

The redemption or entrance fees or fines, in the
case of the Regulated Companies, constantly were,
or could be construed as, a grievance by outsiders
who were determined to find a grievance.   The fines
which the Adventurers exacted in early days, led,
as has been seen, to the Act of 1496, and to the

---

[1] Macpherson (*ut sup.*), vol. ii, p. 432, says they 'removed their
foreign residence or comptoir from Delft to Dort in 1647', but the
petition of 1652 shows that they were then at Rotterdam.

[2] How extensive were the privileges enjoyed by the company in the
Netherlands is shown by the following statement made in a pamphlet
of 1701 : 'The Merchant Adventurers of England, by treaties between
the kings of this realm, and the States General, are exempt from all
customs established by their books of rates, as to clothes, bays, and
serges, to which all other are liable ; and all goods belonging to the
said company, pass through those countries free, by land or water,
free from all tolls and impositions whatsoever, due to any city, town,
or royalty of any Lord ; and their factory are exempt from paying
any public excises, taxes for watch and ward, quarter of soldiers, the
poll tax, the hundred or thousand penny, commonly imposed upon
their own subjects.'   From *A Dialogue between Mr. Smith, Monsieur
Ragouse, Menheir Dorveil, and Mr. Manoel Texiera.*   Anon., 1701,
p. 24.

admission fee being fixed at ten marks, translated into £6 13*s*. 4*d*. It is very difficult to discover what were the exact variations of this redemption or membership fee from time to time. In a statement drawn up after the Hamburg company had been finally dissolved, it is said plainly that the Adventurers were ‘ at first permitted to exact only ten marks, or £6 13*s*. 4*d*., for admission, but subsequently to increase this sum to £50, and afterwards to £100 ’.[1] The fee was fixed at £50 for merchants of London, shipping from the port of London, and £25 for merchants of and shipping from the outports, by King Charles I's Proclamation of 1634 ; but it was doubled, to £100 and £50, by the Lords and Commons Ordinance of 1643. But before these two dates, at the beginning of the seventeenth century, the fee stood as high as £200 ;[2] and the words of the charter of 1564, which have been quoted above,[3] must be construed as allowing the fellowship to fix whatever fee they pleased. The Proclamation of Charles II in April 1663, which gave them back their monopoly, at the same time cut down the membership fee to 20 and 10 marks, £13 6*s*. 8*d*. and £6 13*s*. 4*d*. If a state-

---

[1] *Hamburgh Complaints*, H. of C. Paper 181, 20 April 1835, p. 3.

[2] Wheeler's *Laws, Customs, and Ordinances of the Fellowship of Merchants Adventurers of the Realm of England*, 1608 [B. M. Add. MSS. 18913 Cap. II, pp. 24–5], show that the redemption fee was £200 at the beginning of the seventeenth century (see Dr. Lingelbach's *Internal Organization of the Merchant Adventurers of England, ut sup.*, p. 25).

[3] See above, p. 79.

ment in the West Country protest of or about the year 1670 is to be believed, the fee then stood again at £100 [1] ; and yet once more, another pamphlet, apparently of the very end of the seventeenth century, states that the Hamburg company voluntarily reduced their fee of admission from £13 6s. 8d. to 40s.[2] With regard to the fee charged in the latter part of the eighteenth century, Adam Smith makes the general statement, 'The terms of admission into the Hamburg company are now said to be quite easy'.[3]

The Hamburg company in the eighteenth century.
When Adam Smith wrote, the name Merchant Adventurers had died out, and the company was known only as the Hamburg company. It had become, as compared with its past, a local company, a company of English merchants trading with Germany alone through the one port of Hamburg, and domiciled at Hamburg. At the present day it is difficult to realize that in past times Germany was the one land in Western Europe to which Englishmen could trade with practical certainty of friendship and peace. It was not so with the Netherlands. If the Dutch were not fighting England on their own account, they were always liable

---

[1] *The Reasons humbly offered*, &c. (*ut sup.*), p. 7.

[2] Pamphlet entitled *The charge of companies of merchants more equally borne by impositions on trade than fines for admissions.* It refers to the Act of 1672 (dating it 1673), which reduced the fee of the Eastland Company from £20 to 40s. (see below, p. 175), and was apparently written about 1700 (B.M. 816 m. $\frac{11}{119}$).

[3] *Wealth of Nations*, Bk. V, chap. i, Pt. III, Article I. The *Wealth of Nations* was published in 1776.

to be drawn into war against her. The accession
of a line of German kings to the throne of Great
Britain may well have tended to make the Adventurers gravitate wholly to Germany; that they
gained substantial advantage from being subjects
of a king who was also Elector of Hanover is
shown by the fact that, in 1740, British ships were
exempted from the tolls levied at Stade on vessels
coming up the Elbe—Stade, in the duchy of
Bremen, being under Hanoverian sovereignty.[1]

So they settled down at their single mart at Hamburg, enjoying the extraordinary privileges
conceded to them by the contract of 1618, greater
privileges than were possessed by the citizens of
Hamburg themselves.[2] Exempt alike from military
duties and from civil imposts, having civil jurisdiction among themselves, and in cases in which
aliens were concerned, if the aliens preferred their
courts to those of Hamburg; having criminal jurisdiction among themselves, except in serious crimes—
murder, adultery, and the like; having the 'English
house' provided and kept up for them, they were
in a most enviable position; and if, as we are told,
they were not popular, it could hardly be expected
that aliens so favoured would be liked by the

(marginal note: Their position at Hamburg.)

---

[1] Macpherson, vol. iii, p. 225.
[2] See Dr. Lingelbach's most excellent account of *The Merchant
Adventurers at Hamburg*, *American Historical Review*, vol. ix, 1903-4
(*ut sup.*). He says (pp. 276-7): 'The position of the society at Hamburg was very much that of a state within a state.' He also says
that the Adventurers were not popular at Hamburg.

community at large. 'The English merchants in particular, having extraordinary privileges granted them from this city . . . make a great figure here, different from those of all other nations : they appear as a body with particular jurisdiction and power among themselves. And as they are called in London the Hamburgh company, so they are called at Hamburgh the English hanse or society.'[1] There was no restriction on the goods that they imported into Germany and sold at their quarterly marts, though their cloth trade was, in accordance with the agreement and with the traditions of the fellowship, purely a wholesale trade; and from Hamburg they sent their wares into Upper Germany, to fairs at Leipsic, Frankfort, and other centres. Though no longer in any sense what they had once been, 'The English nation beyond the sea,' at Hamburg they still retained some remnant of their former greatness. But it was a remnant only. Through the eighteenth century the average number of Adventurers resident at Hamburg was very small[2] : the volume of their trade decreased:

[1] Postlethwayt, *Universal Dictionary of Trade and Commerce*, 4th ed., 1774, under 'Hamburg'. The writer tells us 'this factory is incorporated into a company, consisting of 13 members, a governor, and deputy governor'.

[2] Dr. Lingelbach in *The Merchant Adventurers at Hamburg* (*ut sup.*), p. 279 note, shows that in the eighteenth century the average membership at Hamburg was under twenty. He says (p. 280) that during the late period of the Adventurers' history the governor of the fellowship was usually not resident abroad. On the other hand, Postlethwayt writes 'The English are pretty numerous here'.

they became a small clique of merchants, whose
privileges were a survival of greatness long past.
The account given of the British factory at Hamburg, after it had ceased to exist, is that the factory
' at its dissolution, and for many years previous,
had become entirely a close institution '.[1]

The end came as the result of the Napoleonic
Wars. After Jena and Auerstadt, in November,
1806, French troops under Mortier took possession
of the free city of Hamburg. It was not likely
that Napoleon would tolerate the privileged existence
of an English trading company in the great commercial town of the Elbe. Under French pressure
the merchants were compelled to resign to the
Hamburg Senate all their special and exterritorial
rights, to remain in Hamburg only on condition
of becoming citizens of Hamburg. The renuncia-
tion was finally completed in 1808 : the factory
was abolished and the company was dissolved,[2] the
final agreement of April 20, 1808, between the
resident members of the English company and the
Senate of Hamburg, referring to ' the Court master
and Treasurer of The Right Worshipful company
of Merchants Adventurers of England residing in
Hamburg '[3] —a final echo from bygone years. Thus
after a life of four centuries at the least, the Merchant Adventurers of England became a memory—
a splendid memory of the past.

*The end
of the
company.*

[1] *Hamburgh Complaints (ut sup.)*, p. 59.
[2] Ibid., pp. 24–8.   [3] Ibid., p. 28.

The foreign sphere of the Merchant Adventurers.

It has been seen that the sphere of the company's activities beyond the seas was, until the later years of the sixteenth century, Flanders and Brabant, with Calais, at any rate as long as Calais was in English hands and possibly afterwards, on the southern side, the towns of Zeeland and Holland on the north ; that subsequently their marts were confined to the Dutch cities and to Hamburg, and finally to Hamburg alone.   Wheeler defined their area in 1601 in the following words : 'The parts and places which they trade unto are the towns and ports lying between the rivers of Somme in France and the Scawe in the German Sea.'[1]   From the mention of Lübeck in the preamble of the charter of 1564, it is clear that the Adventurers at that date either traded or contemplated trading within the Sound, and the charter in effect confined them to the North Sea, so far as exclusive rights were concerned.   On the other hand, under the terms of the later Eastland Company's charter of 1579, the two companies were given concurrent rights of trading in the lands between the Elbe and the Oder.[2]

Their sphere at home.

At home it would seem that Adventurers, or groups of Adventurers, were at one time or another

[1] p. 23.
[2] For the Eastland charter, see below, pp. 162-6.   The places mentioned in that charter as being open to both companies were Denmark (with the exception of Copenhagen and Elsinore), Mecklenburg, Jutland, Silesia, Moravia, Lübeck, Wismar, Rostock, Stetin, Stralsund, and all the river Oder.

to be found in most of the large commercial centres
of England, at any rate in those which were on or
near the sea. 'The company of Merchants Adventurers', wrote Wheeler, 'consisteth of a great
number of wealthy and well experimented merchants, dwelling in divers great cities, maritime
towns, and other parts of the realm, to wit in
London, York, Norwich, Exeter, Ipswich, Newcastle,
Hull, &c. These men of old time linked and bound
themselves together in company, for the exercise of
merchandise and seafare, trading in cloth kersye
and all other as well English as foreign commodities vendible abroad.' [1] They formed strong bodies
in various cities, as is shown by the Records of the
Company at Newcastle-upon-Tyne,[2] but their main
strength was in London ; and outside London,
Newcastle, York, Hull, and Exeter seem to be the
only cities whose names are as a rule mentioned
in the documents bearing on the subject. Further
reference will presently be made to this point.

The internal organization of the company has Member-
been admirably analysed and described by Dr. Lin- ship and internal
gelbach in the *Transactions of the Royal Historical* organiza-
Society.[3] We have seen that, unlike the Staplers, tion.

---

[1] p. 22.

[2] See *Extracts from the Records of the Merchant Adventurers of Newcastle-upon-Tyne*, edited for the Surtees Society by F. W. Dendy,
1895, &c.

[3] *ut sup., Transactions of the Royal Historical Society*, xvi, 1902.
Dr. Lingelbach's paper, for which he has consulted, among many
sources of information, Wheeler's collection of *The Laws, Customs, and
ordinances of the Fellowship of Merchants Adventurers of the Realm of*

the Merchant Adventurers were rigidly and exclusively Englishmen.[1] Further, they were required
to be merchants in the strict sense of the term, wholesale merchants not shopkeepers. The members,
other than honorary members, obtained the freedom
of the fellowship by patrimony or by apprenticeship—the normal term of apprenticeship being
eight years—or by payment of the redemption fee
which ruled from time to time. The words already
quoted from the charter of 1564, ' conditions and
distinctions and diversity in freedom ', are evidence
of the fact that there were degrees of privileges,
that the members did not all stand on one and the
same footing. Length of years in the fellowship
brought with it additional rights ; and, moreover,
there was a distinction drawn between what were
called the Old and the New Hanse, the old Hanse
including those whose forbears had been members
of the company, before the entrance fee was reduced
by the Act of 1496. Old and New Hanse together
formed a most powerful corporation, envied and at
times bitterly hated by outsiders, English and Germans alike, monopolists no doubt, but never uncon-
trolled monopolists, doing England's early work
beyond the seas more effectively than if the carry-

England (1608, B.M. Add. MSS. 18913), is a most able and lucid
analysis of a very difficult subject.

[1] See above, p. 79. In Rymer, under date 15 February 1633,
1632 o.s., will be found a licence to the governor and fellowship of
Merchant Adventurers to readmit four men who had been dis-
franchised for marrying foreigners.

ing of her cloth to foreign markets had been left to be 'a promiscuous straggling and dispersed trade'.[1]

All the members swore on admission an oath of allegiance to the company, to be 'obedient and assisting to the governor, his deputy or deputies, and assistants of the Fellowship of Merchant Adventurers in the parts of Holland, Zeeland, Brabant, Flanders, and within the Crown and marches of Calais, as also in East Frieseland or any other countries or place on this side the seas where the company is and shall be privileged'; and there was a special proviso for apprentices in the following terms, which testify to varieties in the terms of membership : 'Provided that you shall not enjoy the benefit of this your freedom, but if you serve your master well and truly according to your indenture, or else that you be set over to some other person freeman of this fellowship coming in by the same Hanse that your first master was made free by, and serve eight years complete at the least, or else this oath which you have taken is to be void.'[2] *The oath of membership.*

The governing body to which the members swore allegiance, and which was first constituted by Henry VII's charter of 1505, consisted of a gover- *The governing body and its headquarters.*

[1] Wheeler, p. 13, 'For this vent of wool and woollen wares (the principal commodities of the realm) it is most profitable both for the Prince and country to use a governed company, and not to permit a promiscuous straggling and dispersed trade'.

[2] Dendy, *ut sup.*, vol. ii, p. 18. Cf. Lingelbach, *Internal Organization, &c.*, pp. 30–1. In the version of the oath given by Lingelbach for the words 'on this side the seas' is read 'on this and that side the seas'.

nor and twenty-four assistants, in whose hands was
full authority, legislative, administrative, and judicial. They were elected by the General Court of the
fellowship, that is by the whole body of the members at the principal mart for the time being, and
to this Governing Body and the General Court,
both alike domiciled beyond the seas, all the
Merchant Adventurers of England, and all the
groups of Merchant Adventurers of England, in
all the towns where such groups existed, whether
in England or abroad, were subordinate, even in
the matter of appointing their own local officers.
As late as 1720 we read, 'This company is governed
according to their charter, by the major part of the
said Fellowship residing beyond the seas ; where
annually in the month of June, they elect out of
the fellowship a governor, and deputy governors,
for all their other residencies and courts, both in
those foreign parts and within England, as at
London, York, Hull, Newcastle, &c.' [1]   Not in

[1] Strype, *ut sup.*, vol. ii, Bk. V, p. 260. Hamburg is said to be then
'the chief court of all the Fellowship, residing both in England and
beyond the seas '. Wheeler, writing more than a century earlier, is
equally clear. ' The said company hath a governor, or in his absence
a deputy, and four and twenty assistants in the mart town who have
jurisdiction and full authority, as well from Her Majesty, as from the
princes states and rulers of the Low Countries, and beyond the seas,
without appeal. . . . By the said governor and assistants are also
appointed and chosen a deputy, and certain discreet persons, to be
associates to the said deputy in all other places convenient as well
within as without the realm of England, who all hold correspondence
with the Governor of the Company, and chief Court in the mart town
on the other side the seas and have subaltern power . . .' (p. 30). See
Lingelbach, who argues out the question very exhaustively.

London, not in England, but beyond the seas were
the head-quarters of the fellowship, wherever the
main mart was established at the time, at Bruges,
at Antwerp, at Middelburg, at Hamburg. Not
within the realm but outside it, save only when
Calais was an English port and for a space the
Adventurers made it their centre, or the king made
it for them, on foreign soil not on English ground,
was the seat of government of 'the English nation
beyond the sea'. So it had been more or lessfrom
the beginning : the original grant of Henry IV was
not a charter to incorporate an English company
in England : it was in so many words a grant for
the better government of English merchants remaining and sojourning in the Netherlands, Brabant,
and Flanders, to ensure order and justice among
them, to remedy and prevent abuses. No such
extensive powers as are given in the grant would
have been needed within the realm. There was
this advantage too in having the ultimate source of
authority on the other side of the Channel, that
thereby no one English city was set over another.
The company, it may be said in paradoxical truth,
maintained its national character by keeping its
rulers expatriated. Had the seat of government
been in an English city, the Merchant Adventurers
of England might in public estimation have been
narrowed and localized.

Even as things were, the charge was freely made
that the fellowship was in effect a London company.

What truth was there in this charge? What position did London actually hold in the fellowship? In order to answer these questions we must further consider two other questions. Were all those who styled themselves Merchant Adventurers in the various cities of England members of the company of the Merchant Adventurers of England? and Was the company of Merchant Adventurers of England, in fact as in name, a unitary company or was it a federation of companies?

The English homes of the Merchant Adventurers.

English traders with the Low Countries and Germany would naturally be found mainly on the Eastern side of England, facing the Channel and the North Sea ; and Wheeler's list of English cities wherein Merchant Adventurers dwelt, which has been quoted above, includes only one town—Exeter —in the West or South-west of England. Bristol is conspicuous by its absence from the list. The names which keep recurring as homes of Merchant Adventurers of England, are, as has been stated, London, Newcastle, York, Hull, and Exeter. It may therefore be assumed that at these centres the company had at one time or another the strongest following, though there were no doubt members of the company not only in the other towns which Wheeler names, but also at Leeds, for instance, and probably in most cities of the kingdom which had any considerable cloth industry. On the other hand, it by no means follows that all Merchant Adventurers were members of the fellowship of the

Merchant Adventurers of England, or that, where-
ever there were members of the fellowship, there
was a local branch or court established. Some light
is given by comparing the conditions of three provincial cities—two, Bristol and Exeter, in the West
and South-west of England; one in the North,
Newcastle-upon-Tyne.

'The Master Wardens and Commonalty of Mer- The Merchant Venturers of the City of Bristol' were Venturers
incorporated by charter of Edward VI in 1552, of Bristol.
the charter being subsequently confirmed by Act
of Parliament in 1565. A clause in this charter
provided that the statutes which should be made
under it should not be prejudicial to ' our well
beloved subjects the Governor Assistants and Society
of Merchants commonly called Merchant Adventurers, going into and frequenting the coast of
Holland Zeeland Brabant and Flanders and other
regions lands and dominions to the same parts
adjoining '. This proviso was repeated in another
charter given to the Bristol company by Charles I
in 1639; but four years later, in 1643, King Charles
gave a new charter empowering the Merchant Adventurers of Bristol to trade freely into places where
other companies operated, including ' the company
of Merchant Adventurers of London '. It is clear,
therefore, that the Merchant Venturers of the City
of Bristol were entirely distinct from the fellowship
of Merchant Adventurers of England. There may
well have been members of the latter fellowship

living at Bristol, but there is no sign of any local court of the fellowship, and the Bristol society was a wholly independent body. This was only what might be expected. Although Bristol was a great centre of the cloth industry, yet Bristol shipping was not directed to the Low Countries. The overseas trade of Bristol was with Ireland, with Scandinavia, with Bordeaux, and Spain, north and south of the sphere of the Merchant Adventurers of England. Bristol was no doubt jealous of London, and in 1669 the Bristol Adventurers tried—though vainly—to induce the Newcastle Adventurers to combine against the Merchant Adventurers of England on account of their London connexion;[1] but it is Exeter, not Bristol, that figures in the manifold West Country complaints against the great company. The interests of the Bristol Merchant Adventurers did not as a rule collide with those of the Merchant Adventurers of England, and the two corporations were wholly independent of each other.

The Merchant Adventurers of Exeter.

A charter of Queen Elizabeth, granted in the year 1560, and possibly renewing an older charter of 1556, incorporated the 'Governor Consuls and Society of Merchants Adventurers of the City of Exeter, trafficking the realm of France and dominions of the French King', who were empowered to make laws for their trade and society not repugnant to the laws of

[1] See Dendy, *ut sup.*, pp. 136-7, and Preface p. xviii. The above account has been mainly taken from *The History of the Merchant Venturers of the City of Bristol*, by John Latimer, 1903.

England. No citizen of the city or county of Exeter was to be allowed to trade with France, unless he was a member of the society. The trade was with Spain as well as France, until a separate guild was established to deal with the Spanish trade, and the Society apparently came to an end in the course of the Civil War in the seventeenth century.[1] From this it would seem that the Merchant Adventurers of Exeter, as would be expected in the case of a South-western port, were mainly concerned with trading into regions south of the sphere of the Merchant Adventurers of England ; and so far, like the Bristol Adventurers, they would be wholly independent of the Merchant Adventurers of England. But Exeter, as has been seen, figures as one of the chief provincial centres of the Merchant Adventurers of England ; though it was a centre where the Merchant Adventurers' following died away in the course of the seventeenth century. In a statement by the representatives of the great company, in the year 1661, we are told 'Exeter once had one of their most considerable courts in it, though now there be only one member there',[2] and presumably the hostility of the Exeter merchants to the Merchant Adventurers of England resulted from or

[1] Taken from *An Elizabethan Guild of the City of Exeter, an account of the proceedings of the Society of Merchant Adventurers during the latter half of the sixteenth century*, by William Cotton, 1873. The Exeter charter was subsequently safeguarded by Act of Parliament, 4 Jac. I, cap. 9.

[2] Quoted in substance by Anderson ii. 118, and by Macpherson ii. 501.

coincided with the decay and extinction in the city of the local branch of the fellowship. The Exeter merchants, in short, all gradually came into the category of free traders or interlopers, fighting a monopoly of which they had once partaken. The case of Exeter, then, resembled that of Bristol, in that the group of Merchant Adventurers in the city who obtained a royal charter, and therefore stand out as the typical Merchant Adventurers of Exeter, were in their sphere of operations wholly outside the area covered by the Merchant Adventurers of England, and therefore presumably had no lot or part with the Merchant Adventurers of England. On the other hand, it differed from that of Bristol in that it was at one time the seat of a local court of the Merchant Adventurers of England, a court which, it must be assumed, was wholly distinct from the Governor, Consuls, and Society of Merchants Adventurers of Exeter trading to France, though it is more than likely that the two bodies were largely composed of the same merchants.

The Merchant Adventurers of Newcastle-upon-Tyne.

In 1547 King Edward VI gave a charter to 'the Merchants Adventurers inhabiting within the said town and the county of the same said town of Newcastle who now are of the Fellowship of Merchants Venturers in Brabant in the parts of beyond the seas', incorporating them under the title of 'Governor Assistants Wardens and Fellowship of Merchant Venturers inhabiting within the foresaid

town and county of the town of Newcastle-upon-
Tyne '. They were empowered to make ordinances
' only concerning those who are or shall be of the
same fellowship '. This charter was confirmed by
Queen Mary in 1553 and Queen Elizabeth in 1559.
The Bristol charter incorporated a body of Merchant
Adventurers whom the terms of the charter prove
to have been a body wholly independent of and
distinct from the Merchant Adventurers of England.
The Exeter charter incorporated a body of Merchant
Adventurers who, it must be inferred from the
direction of their trade, were also independent of
the Merchant Adventurers of England; but by
their side in the same city was a Court of the
Merchant Adventurers of England. The case of
Newcastle-upon-Tyne was entirely different from
that of the other two cities. Here the local body of
Merchant Adventurers, which was incorporated by
royal charter, was composed exclusively of members
of the fellowship of Merchant Adventurers of England. Looking straight across the North Sea,
Newcastle traded with the Low Countries and
Germany, the field of the Merchant Adventurers
of England; it was natural, therefore, that the
Merchant Adventurers of Newcastle should all be
members of the great fellowship. But Newcastle
was at the same time the northernmost commercial
centre in England, the farthest from London. Its
special position as the outlet of the far north of
England was recognized by the royal licences and

the laws which exempted Newcastle citizens from
the rule as to shipping staple goods to Calais ;
here, therefore, if anywhere, there was likely to
be resistance to any claim on the part of London
to override local independence in matters of trade.
From the records of the Merchant Adventurers of
Newcastle we gain some light as to whether the
fellowship of Merchant Adventurers of England
was a unitary body or a federation, and as to the
position which London held in the fellowship.

The
dispute
between
the Mer-
chant
Adven-
turers of
New-
castle-
upon-
Tyne and
the
govern-
ing body
of the
fellow-
ship.
In 1519—it would seem because the Merchant
Adventurers at Newcastle were at the time weak
and struggling—the main company agreed to accept
the sum of £8 per annum from the body at Newcastle in composition for certain dues payable by
the individual members.   This was before the local
charter had been obtained, but the arrangement
continued after that date until, in 1623, the governing body of the Merchant Adventurers of England
decided that the Newcastle Adventurers must pay
on the same footing as the members of the fellowship at York, Hull, and elsewhere.   There then
ensued a controversy, protracted over many years,
carried up to the highest authorities in the land, into
the merits of which it is not necessary to enter
beyond noting the position taken up by either
party.   The Newcastle Adventurers contended in
effect that the fellowship of Merchant Adventurers
of England was a federation, that the local bodies
were independent one of another, and that the

source of their complaint was an attempt on the part of the Merchant Adventurers of London to dominate their brethren in Newcastle. In 1654, addressing the Lord Protector Cromwell, they maintained 'That the Merchant Adventurers of England consist of divers companies inhabiting in divers other parts of England as well as in the city of London, and each of them by the law of England declared in Parliament ought to have free trade and not to be charged without their consent by any of the other with any exaction, fine, imposition, extortion or contribution whatsoever'.[1] In the course of the controversy they spoke of their Newcastle Society as 'a several and distinct company'[2]; they laid stress upon having to support their own government as well as to contribute to the general fellowship; they pointed to their charter as evidence of their separate corporate existence; and they charged the Merchant Adventurers of London with having usurped the name of Merchant Adventurers of England.

On the other side, the governing body of the Merchant Adventurers of England were very explicit in maintaining a diametrically opposite standpoint. Here is their contention in 1637, formulated for the King and his Council. 'That they were not styled Merchant Adventurers of London, as the parties term them, but Merchants Adventurers of England, and were in these times dispersed and

[1] Dendy, *ut sup.*, vol. ii, p. 57.   [2] Dendy, vol. ii, p. 58.

dwelt as well in the outports of this kingdom, viz.
at York, Hull, Exeter, and Newcastle, as at London,
though the greatest number always dwelt at London,
but all of them so dispersed were sworn to be
subject to one and the same government of trade
and to such orders as should be made by the head
court of their Society, which ever was and yet is
beyond seas, and not at London.'[1] In answer to
the Newcastle representation to the Lord Protector
in 1654 they wrote : 'It is denied that the said
fellowship ever did or now doth consist of divers
companies inhabiting in divers other parts of
England, either in the City of London or anywhere
else, much less in Newcastle.'[2] In their correspondence they refused to recognize the governor
of the Newcastle guild. 'We find by our charter
there can be but one governor, though divers
deputies of the fellowship of Merchants Adventurers of England.'[3] So they laid down the position
in 1637, and in 1656, asserting that they had some
years before assigned to Newcastle a deputy and
subordinate court of the fellowship, as at York
and Hull, which Newcastle had declined to accept,
they announced that they would now deal with
Newcastle only 'as a generality of freemen of the
Fellowship of Merchants Adventurers of England
there residing'.[4] At a later date they took steps
for setting up a new organization at Newcastle to

[1] Dendy, vol. ii, p. 19.   [2] Ibid., p. 59.
[3] Ibid., p. 7.   [4] Ibid., p. 66.

supplant the recalcitrant Merchant Adventurers guild in that city.[1]

Here, then, were two opposite views of the basis upon which the Merchant Adventurers' Fellowship rested. There was the Newcastle view that it was a federation of coequal corporate bodies, and that what purported to be the central body was only the London company usurping authority over other kindred and federated associations. On the other hand, there was the view held and enunciated with the clearest emphasis by the representatives and spokesmen of the main body, that the Merchant Adventurers of England were Adventurers of England not of London, that they were one company not a federation of companies, and that any local organization within the fellowship, whether in London or any other English centre, possessed only such authority as was delegated to it by the central government ruling from beyond the seas. It cannot be doubted that in principle the latter view was the true one. The fellowship was one, a national fellowship, not the creature of any one English city; a fellowship claiming the allegiance of individual members, not a federation of independent groups. But it must at the same time be admitted that there was room for the two contradictory views so long as kings and queens gave charters which might conflict with each other. The Newcastle Guild of Merchant Adventurers derived

The fellowship of Merchant Adventurers of England was in principle one company not a federation.

[1] Ibid., p. 107.

its authority from the same royal source as the Fellowship of Merchant Adventurers of England. Their governor was not in fact a mere deputy of the Governor of the Merchant Adventurers of England, he held office in virtue of a royal charter, equally valid with the provisions which empowered the Merchant Adventurers of England to create local courts and deputies of the fellowship. The truth is that during the long life of the Merchant Adventurers there were and must have been from time to time modifications of system and diverse interpretations of provisions and precedents; nor is it reasonable to look for clearly defined lines, consistently and logically upheld through generations, in lieu of gradual change and evolution; none the less the one main outstanding fact is that this great fellowship was in principle one fellowship, and its government was in principle not in an English city but beyond the seas.

But, if it be admitted that the fellowship was one, unitary not federal, it might still have been a London fellowship; and again, if it be admitted that it was not in principle a London fellowship, The posi- it may yet have been so in actual practice. What tion of London in conclusion can fairly be arrived at on these points? the fel- Against the plain and emphatic denial that the lowship. Merchant Adventurers of England were really Merchant Adventurers of London, against the plain and definite assertion, which was not seriously controverted, that the seat of government for the fellowship was beyond the seas, must be set the following facts. London was not only the political and commercial capital of England, it was the birthplace of the Merchant Adventurers of England, who were children of a London guild—the guild of Mercers. The early predominance of the Merchant Adventurers of London is shown by the preamble to the Act of 1496, embodying the protest of 'The Merchant Adventurers inhabiting and dwelling in divers parts of this realm of England out of the City of London' against 'the Fellowship of the Mercers and other Merchants and Adventurers dwelling and being free within the City of London', against 'the said fellowship of Merchants of London and their confederates'.[1] It was allowed that among the Merchant Adventurers of England 'the greatest number always dwelt at London'.[2] The letters patent or charter of Henry VII in January 1506 gave the governor power to call 'Courts and Congregations of all our Merchant Adventurers as well within our City of London at the place of old accustomed as elsewhere', and a clause in almost the same words was included in Queen Elizabeth's charter of 1564.[3] When the Merchant Adventurers in November 1653, at the time of the first Dutch war, laid before the Council of State the articles which they wished inserted in whatever treaty might be concluded with the Dutch, one article was to the effect that the Dutch should not prohibit

[1] See above, p. 68.   [2] Ibid., p. 132.   [3] Ibid., pp. 72, 80.

the Adventurers from levying 'such impositions and duties upon the commodities. of their trade, by them imported into or exported out of the said United Provinces of the Netherlands, which by the Fellowship of Merchant Adventurers of England residing in London shall be, for the maintenance of their government, thought fit to be imposed or levied '.[1]

At the beginning of the seventeenth century the volume of trade into and out of the port of London exceeded that of all the outports put together, and we have seen that the exception made in favour of the Staplers and Merchant Adventurers in the Shipping Act of the first year of Queen Elizabeth applied only to sailings from the Thames.[2] The voice of London must naturally have carried much weight at all times. Were representations to be made to King or Parliament, the Londoners, being on the spot, would be the men to make them. In time of war, when the marts beyond the seas were closed or threatened, the fellowship would naturally gravitate to London as its centre. Thus at the time when the Adventurers, in the words just

---

[1] Sec. 9 of the articles. See above, pp. 63, 74, 91 notes.

[2] See above, p. 77, and compare the amount of wool shipped from the port of London in Edward III's reign above, p. 44 note. There were about ten years towards the end of the thirteenth century, in which what were called the new customs were greater at the port of Boston than at that of London; but the tables of import and export duties quoted by Misselden in *The Circle of Commerce* (1623, pp. 121-2 and 127-9) for the years 1613 and 1622, show an enormous preponderance in the customs of the port of London over those of all the other English ports combined.

quoted, spoke of 'the Fellowship of Merchant
Adventurers of England residing in London', the
Dutch war had closed their mart in the Netherlands, and must have crippled their communication
with Hamburg. In war or peace, at all times and
under all circumstances, London must inevitably
have given a lead to the provincial cities, and
Londoners would not have been human had they
not asserted and tried to exercise some measure
of ascendancy.

Moreover, there is definite evidence that London
was on a different footing from the other Merchant
Adventurers' centres in England, that the London
Board at all times specially represented in England
the governing body beyond the seas, and had, at some
times at any rate, a special measure of influence if
not of control in regard to the governing body. In
the Newcastle controversy, for instance, in 1637,
the governing body, writing from Delft or Rotterdam, contended that they 'have done nothing but
what hath been thought reasonable, and was agreed
upon with the joint advice of the Courts at London,
Hambrough, and in this place' ;[1] while a statement
made by the fellowship in vindication of themselves
against outside attacks, in 1661, asserted definitely
that London had an authoritative voice with regard
to the decisions taken at head-quarters. 'They all
meet together in their marts abroad, where their con-
sultations are for the interest of the whole kingdom

[1] Dendy, vol. ii, p. 6.

in the clothing trade, and where a majority of the freemen and traders present governs in all matters. Yet nothing can be concluded in that chief mart town beyond sea, but by the concurrence of that other court which resides in the United Netherlands, and of this here in London. And this court at London maintains a correspondence all along with all other their distinct courts, as of York, Hull and Newcastle.'[1] In 1688 the governing body at Hamburg agreed that London should choose its own deputy, and that the concurrence of London should be obtained in the appointment of the governor of the fellowship, the by-laws which were enacted, and the dues which were levied, though the agreement was not adhered to subsequently.[2] In the matter of the Newcastle dispute, in 1637, the two Lords Chief Justices of England and the Lord Chief Baron, in their report to the Privy Council, referred to the fellowship as 'the Company of London residing beyond the seas';[3] and the charter given to the Merchant Venturers of Bristol by Charles I in 1643 referred to the 'company of Merchant Adventurers of London'.[4] It cannot be doubted either that the majority of overseas members at any given time were Londoners or representatives of London merchants, or again that the court in London had a dominating influence in the fellowship. Take a somewhat

---

[1] Quoted in substance by Anderson, ii. 118, and Macpherson, ii. 501.

[2] Lingelbach, *Internal Organization, &c.*, pp. 54–5. For this Agreement see the end of B.M. Add. MSS. 18913.

[3] Dendy, vol. ii, p. 23.   [4] Above, p. 125.

analogous instance at the present day, the case of
a great bank, the Hongkong and Shanghai Banking
Corporation.   The head-quarters of the Bank are at
Hongkong, but it would be futile to contend that the
office of the Bank in the City of London and the
London board are on the footing of an ordinary
branch office of a bank.[1] The conclusion that the
Merchant Adventurers of England were a national
not a purely London body, and that their seat of
government was beyond the seas, is not vitiated by
admitting what is at once prima facie probable and
proved by undoubted evidence, that London held a
predominant place in the councils of the fellowship.

We have seen that it was from the South-west
of England that the fellowship was most bitterly
and continuously attacked, the attacks emanating
evidently from outside not from inside the company.
It was the old story of angry provincial resentment
against the growing overlordship of the metropolis.
The West Country clothiers sought to overthrow
the Merchant Adventurers of England, not merely
because they were monopolists, but also and mainly
because their monopoly enured to the benefit of
London—' London, the residence of this company
(who ship most of the woollen commodities made
on this side Trent from that port)'.[2] South of the
Trent London was in past times, as it now is,

---

[1] The analogy is not complete, because Hongkong is a British
possession.

[2] From the pamphlet of 1670 (referred to above, pp. 105, 111, 114),
p. i*

geographically the dominating centre, to a greater extent than for the North of England, and the trade with the middle continent from the western districts of England tended to be drawn eastwards to the great port on the Thames. Given a city, at once the political centre of the realm and the greatest mart of commerce, given too the fact that it was most centrally placed for a particular area of overseas trade, and the wonder is that the Merchant Adventurers of England were not exclusively a London company.

Perhaps the case may be read as follows. Down to the time of Henry VII the Merchant Adventurers were almost exclusively Londoners, though, as far as the government of the fellowship, following the trade of the fellowship, was concerned, Londoners sojourning beyond the seas. The Act of 1496, with the lowering of the membership fee, struck at the root of the London monopoly : there ensued the evils which Gresham noted, deterioration of the class of merchants and of the standard of their commodities. Failing to reverse the Act and restore the old order, it would seem that Gresham set himself to effect reform by making the company more avowedly and distinctively a national as opposed to a metropolitan company, and thus the 1564 charter was granted to 'the Merchants Adventurers of England'. To the company standing on this wide basis was conceded power to levy high membership fees and to exclude retail traders—the points which Gresham considered essential in order to restore the status of English cloth and English cloth traders. Thenceforward the Adventurers were in no sense a London company; but the preponderance in number of Londoners among its members, coupled with the early London connexion and the growing relative strength of London, assured to London in any year a special standing in the fellowship.[1]

What place should be assigned to the Merchant Adventurers in English history? What bearing had they upon the Imperial future of England? Have they ever been given their due as pioneers of the great destiny of a great people? Let us sum up the main outstanding features of this memorable company.

If their birth be dated from the grant of 1407, and the claims to an earlier existence be ignored, they had a life of exactly four centuries. The Merchants of the Staple were born before them; in a sense they outlived them; but for the greater part of their history the Staplers were little more than a shadow without a substance. The Merchant Adventurers had a definite, continuous, working life, in one phase or another, from the central years

The longevity of the Merchant Adventurers Company.

---

[1] It is only fair to note that the above view is not supported by an entry in the Journals of the House of Commons for May 5, 1624 (vol. i, p. 698). An opinion was expressed by a member as follows: 'This company like a fruitful tree, as long as governed by parliament; but not since they governed themselves; which was 6 Eliz.; *Before called the Merchant Adventurers of England, now of London.*'

of the Middle Ages till the beginning of the nineteenth century. They began with the House of Lancaster; they ended, as so many institutions ended, in the upheaval of the world at the hands of Napoleon. They ran the course of a full long life in the fullest human sense. They rose, they grew, they flourished and decayed. They saw and they contributed in a marked degree to the evolution of English history. They were themselves a striking illustration of evolution on the lines on which the English race has marched through the centuries. They embodied, to quote Carlyle's words, the English instinct 'to expand, if it be possible, some old habit or method, already found fruitful, into new growth for the new need'.[1] Born of a guild, they became, as a regulated company, a guild enlarged and expanded to meet wider calls than those of a particular trade in an English city: they embodied 'the development of national commerce along lines which were familiar in municipal life'.[2] That continuity, which has been an outstanding feature of English character and English

[1] *Past and Present*, Bk. IV, chap. 3.
[2] *Select Charters of Trading Companies*, A. D. 1530-1707, Selden Society, edited by Cecil T. Carr, Introduction, p. xii. Similarly Dendy (*ut sup.*, vol. ii, Introduction, p. xi) writes, 'The regulated companies were merely a developement of the local guilds adapted for trading purposes beyond the seas'. Adam Smith, in the *Wealth of Nations*, emphasizes the same point: 'Regulated companies resemble, in every respect, the corporation of trades, so common in the cities and towns of all the different countries of Europe, and are a sort of enlarged monopolies of the same kind' (Bk. V, chap. 1, Pt. III, Art. I).

history, was at once illustrated and upheld by the Merchant Adventurers. It was illustrated in their decay as in their growth. Having emerged from a guild into a regulated company, they did not enter upon the further stage of becoming a joint-stock company: a regulated company they were to the end. As they had expanded, so they contracted; as they had grown, so they decayed; with no violent change or cataclysm; flickering out as little more than a small and select English guild in a German city.

The actual beginnings of the Overseas Empire of Great Britain coincided roughly with the beginnings of joint-stock companies, and in the construction of the Empire joint stock played a part which can hardly be over-estimated. It was when companies were formed to carry British commercial enterprise into lands and countries unknown, that the driving power, which comes from combining and organizing financial effort, became needed and appreciated; that private citizens, still doing the work of the State, but doing it in wider, stranger, more distant fields, realized and developed the strength of the common purse. The Merchant Adventurers had no lot or part in voyages to far-off lands: they did not compete with the later companies which sprang from the seed which they had sown. Operating near home in narrower compass than those who came after, and at an earlier stage in history, they fought their fight and won their way in the looser framework of a regulated company.

Regulated and joint-stock companies.

The Merchant Adventurers were a national company.

But for this selfsame reason they were in a more real sense a national company than any of those that came after. They were Merchant Adventurers, not in order to share a common profit but in order to secure a common safeguard for their individual trading. Every man among them, in Wheeler's words, traded apart.[1] 'There are no merchants of the kingdom', wrote Misselden, 'that do more bid, and outbid one another at the market, than they.'[2] Their bond was the wider bond of the guild, not the narrower bond of the joint-stock company : theirs was a common brotherhood, but not a common purse. Each man ran his own risk, each man took his own profit or loss, but they were linked together to uphold a trade in which they all were interested, and that trade was a national trade, the greatest industry of England. The fact that they had members and courts of members at different centres, in this English city and in that, that they were not focused at one English centre alone, that they had their head-quarters in a foreign land, whereby the cardinal fact of their English nationality was emphasized, made them much more 'the English nation beyond the sea' than if they had all been simply shareholders in one concern, which had only one English home, in London. 'They count it their honour', said the spokesmen of the company in answer to their blasphemers in 1661, 'that they

[1] Above, p. 19.
[2] *The Circle of Commerce*, 1623, p. 62.

are no company of one city, Town, or Borough, but a national corporation, and disposed all over the Kingdom.'[1] It has been seen how exclusively English they were, how rigidly it was prescribed that the fundamental basis of membership, English nationality, should not be weakened by foreign ties. It has been seen, too, to what extent these national merchants served national interests and furthered a national policy. It was no idle boast that 'when either the honour of the nation abroad, or the necessities thereof at home, have required the same, this fellowship, because [of] their government was always to be found, were still ready at hand'.[2]

As a national company, not as mere trade rivals, they stand out in their long contest with the German Merchants of the Steelyard; and the measure of their success is to be found in the fact that, while they ousted the Hansards from their privileged position in London, they themselves secured a permanent home in a Hanseatic city, where they retained special privileges, until Frenchmen, not Germans, brought the end. Before the present war British commerce was pressed in a growing degree by German competition : the war itself is a trial of strength between German and British methods : it is well then to recall a time

The Merchant Adventurers and the Hanse Merchants.

---

[1] These words precede the words quoted from the same passage on pp. 137-8, above.

[2] From the pamphlet of ? 1670, *The Advantages of the Kingdom of England, &c.* (*ut sup.*, p. 57), p. 2.

when German merchants predominated in London, with peculiar privileges and rights, courted by English kings, while English merchants were but slowly beginning to feel their feet in their own land. It is well too to recall the sequel: the Merchant Adventurers embodied the rise of the English merchant, the supplanting of the foreigner: they learnt from the German, and they bettered their instruction. The Hanse confederacy declined and fell: the Merchant Adventurers in their turn slowly shrank into senility; but they had done their work, they had found out the machinery which was adapted to the English race, as it grew outwards and onwards, and had handled that machinery with conspicuous success.

The Merchant Adventurers were the pioneers of English chartered companies. The machinery was the chartered company, but the chartered company as modelled by English instinct and character; not the artificial creation of king and ministers, as in France; not the nation under the name of a company, as was the case with the Netherlands East India and West India Companies; but the embodiment of private initiative under the sanction of the State, a working compromise such as the English love, whereby English citizens combined with one another to serve at once their own interests and those of the nation, at times and places and in ways of their own choosing. In these latter days, supposed to be days of greater moral scruple than their predecessors, we fix our eyes too exclusively upon the obvious shortcomings

of chartered companies, the evil things which have
soiled their history, the possibilities which they have
offered for buying and selling the welfare of lands and
of men. We should see straighter, and interpret
English history more correctly, if more was thought
and more was told of these companies as the special
means, whether good or evil, which the English,
above all nations, devised and perfected, on their
own peculiar English lines, for making an Empire.
It should be borne in mind that, after some finality
in expansion had seemed to be obtained, after the
East India Company had been brought to an end,
and the territories of the Hudson Bay Company
had been merged in the Dominion of Canada, there
came to birth, less than forty years ago, a new crop
of chartered companies, and with them came ex-
tension of territory and widening of influence as
never before. To pass a right judgement upon
English chartered companies, Bacon's words must
still be borne in mind : ' I did ever think that
trading in companies is most agreeable to the
English nature, which wanteth that same general
vein of a Republic which runneth in the Dutch
and serveth to them instead of a company.' This
wise man saw truly that the chartered company
appealed to the practical English nature as being
better in the working than the 'general vein of a
Republic'. As the British nation is a democracy
under the forms and in the dress of a monarchy,
so the chartered company, as the English moulded

it, has been the incarnation of private enterprise under State licence and modified State control. With all its defects, the system has had the great merit of elasticity: it has been better adapted to a process of evolution, of continuous growth, than any product of the direct action of the State. Moreover, it has had a further merit. Though, as in the case of the Merchant Adventurers in the seventeenth century, English chartered companies, or their leading members, in times of domestic strife in England, may have allied themselves for the moment with one party or another, they have in their essence, from their nature, and by reason of their interests, in the main stood outside party, they have stood for continuity, and in the lands where they have operated they have not represented a king or a parliament: they have been in fact 'the English nation beyond the sea'. The more the overseas history of Great Britain is studied, the more potent this machinery of chartered companies is seen to be—as handled by Englishmen; and the pioneers of it all were the Merchant Adventurers of England. 'Out of it', wrote Wheeler of the fellowship, '(as out of a plentiful nursery) have sprung and proceeded almost all the principal merchants of this realm; at least such companies as have arisen since, have for the most part, fetched their light, pattern, and form of policy and trade from the said society to the inestimable good and commoditie of this realm,

our native country.'[1] When he wrote in 1601, the
great Tudor companies had come to birth ; but, had
he written in later days, the children who came
forth from the nursery would have astounded him
as much by their number as by their growth.
In good truth his company was a plentiful
nursery, for the forerunner and ancestor of all the
chartered companies was the fellowship of the
Merchant Adventurers : they made the first experi-
ments and took the first risks : ' one day still being
a schoolmaster unto the other',[2] they gradually
evolved the machine which built up the British
Empire.

The first embryo of the chartered company is no
less important and no less interesting, in its bearing
upon the Empire that was to be, than the growth
and evolution of the system. We have seen of
what sort was the earliest charter to the Merchant
Adventurers.'[3] It was not a charter to give a trade
monopoly, it was a charter to grant a constitution,
a charter to enable Englishmen sojourning in foreign
parts to govern themselves. The preamble sets forth
the mischief that has occurred and is likely to grow,
' through want of good and discreet rule and government', unless the king intervenes ' for the procuring
of better government'. With this end in view, the
charter prescribes that the merchants ' may freely
and lawfully assemble and meet together', when

The first charter of the Merchant Adven- turers.

The be- ginning of self- govern- ment beyond the seas.

---

[1] Wheeler, pp. 6-7. [2] Ibid., p. 29.
[3] For the charter, see Appendix.

and where they please, to elect governors ' in those parts at their good liking '. The governors are empowered to rule and administer justice to all English merchants resorting to those parts, to adjust disputes among the English merchants themselves, and disputes between English merchants and the merchants of the soil, to punish, to enforce, ' and by the common consent of the aforesaid merchants our subjects, to make and establish statutes, ordinances and customs as shall seem expedient in that behalf for the better government of the state of the said merchants our subjects '. There is no word of incorporation, no mention of trading rights or monopolies, no reference to trade in any form, except that merchants are specified. The one and only object of the charter is better government, and the way in which better government is to be attained is by granting self-government. The king knew well, and the merchants knew well, that, given law and order, English trade would prosper without government assistance; regulated companies were the early companies, regulated trade is what they stood for, as opposed to promiscuous and disorderly traffic. The king knew well, and the merchants knew well, that among Englishmen the golden road to law and order is to give them definite authority to govern themselves, to choose their own rulers and make their own laws. Exactly two hundred years later, in 1606, the continuous history of the British Empire beyond the

seas began with the grant of a royal charter to the
Virginia Company ; the charter which was given
to the English merchants in the Low Countries for
their better government in 1407 might almost have
been a model for the founding of English colonies
in America.

There were these two points of difference. The
Merchant Adventurers were temporary colonists,
sojourners only. The charter of 1564, intent on
preserving the English citizenship of Englishmen
in foreign parts, placed a ban on the Adventurer
who 'shall for himself or for his wife inhabit out
of the said realm'. Further, they were sojourners
in the dominions of Christian princes : they held
their tenure there—to quote the charter again—
'according to the privileges and authorities granted
unto them by the Lords or Governors of the parts
aforesaid'. Like the German merchants in London,
they acquired in some sort ex-territorial privileges,
and to regulate this little *imperium in imperio* the
English king gave them their charter. When
nations were not fully consolidated, when national
governments were in their infancy, small communities within larger communities were the order of
the day ; the Statute of the Staple constituted
such a body in England itself. But the record
of ex-territorial rights in the story of the British
Empire is of unique interest as illustrating the strain
of continuity, the perpetual evolution which has
marked English history. In the beginning extra-

The beginning of ex-territorial privileges.

ordinary privileges in foreign parts were given by
the rulers of those parts to English citizens, and
the English kings recognized those privileges and
delegated to the possessors of them powers of
government and jurisdiction. English citizens went
on into further foreign parts, outside Christendom,
and, at Constantinople in particular, ex-territorial
rights grew up. Then the British government, as
the centuries went on, took up the rights which
their subjects had acquired, and exercised them
directly on their behalf. Thus, in the words of the
Foreign Jurisdiction Act, ' by treaty, capitulation,
grant, usage, sufferance, and other lawful means
His Majesty the King has jurisdiction within divers
foreign countries'. British citizens went on yet
further, into lands where no government was known,
and by this same Foreign Jurisdiction Act ' where
a foreign country is not subject to any government
from whom His Majesty the King might obtain
jurisdiction in the manner recited by this act, His
Majesty shall by virtue of this act have jurisdiction
over His Majesty's subjects for the time being resident in or resorting to that country '. Students of the
history of the British Empire know well how potent
and far-reaching has been the application of this
provision, how it has operated in the Protectorates,
bringing rule under the guise of protection, it may
be in Pacific islands, it may be in the continental
areas of Central Africa. The seeds of it were in
bygone times, when there were English Merchant

Adventurers resident in or resorting to Brabant and Flanders.[1]

When the Merchant Adventurers were persecuted, Welcome or threatened with persecution, in one city, they fled given to to another; but such persecution or restraint of the Mer- chant trade as fell to their lot emanated not so much from Adven- the cities themselves as from the political overlords turers in foreign of the cities for the time being. It is most note- cities. worthy how, with rare exceptions, one foreign city after another coveted their presence, and urged their return. 'Procession and great joy' attended their return to Antwerp in Henry VII's reign. Emden was at pains to explain that the Emperor Rudolf's prohibition was not the doing of Emden. Stade wanted them back again. Time and again Bruges would have had them back. 'In man's memory', writes Wheeler, 'they proffered a great sum of money unto the said merchants, with offer of more ample privileges and immunities than ever they had before in Bridges, or anywhere else, yea in a man- ner they proffered a blank to tie them to what the English thought good to have the traffic again in their town.'[2] So it had been before Wheeler's

---

[1] See the very interesting note on p. xliii of the Introduction to *Early Voyages and Travels in the Levant* (Hakluyt Soc. Series, 1893), in which Mr. Albert Gray, K.C., C.B., now President of the Hakluyt Society, traces the Foreign Jurisdiction Act from the Act of 1825, which wound up the Levant Company and transferred the duties which had been performed by the Company's consuls to government officers.

[2] p. 16. See the attestations from various cities in favour of the Adventurers printed at the end of Wheeler's book. See also Parker's

time, so it was in later years. Bruges wanted the
English back at almost any price. It was only
under pressure from the French that Hamburg
cancelled their privileges. Is there any such continuous evidence in favour of merchants of other
nations? Yet the English have never been an
ingratiating race, never popular in the ordinary
sense. These merchants created in the cities where
they sojourned, wealth, employment, industrial and
financial prosperity, and therefore, with reason
they were welcome. But why did these good
things come in their train? Because they ex-
hibited and developed the special qualities and
characteristics, difficult to analyse and to define,
which afterwards ensured to their countrymen, as
traders and as colonists, permanence and success in
wider and more distant fields. We read of them
at Hamburg that ' their judgements are so just and
summary, that the burghers generally make application to them, when they have demands upon any
of the British factory, preferring their decisions to
any other court in the jurisdiction of the city'.
As at Hamburg in the eighteenth century, so long
before in the Low Countries, and so in lands which
the Merchant Adventurers never knew, in India or
in China, the peoples of the soil trusted, even if

Discourse concerning Freedom of Trade (ut sup.). Allowing for exag-
geration on behalf of partisans of the fellowship, there is incon-
testable evidence of the value attached to the presence of the
Merchant Adventurers by the foreign cities.

[1] Postlethwayt (*ut sup.*), s.v. Hamburg.

they did not like, the English. There has been in them something more than mere capacity for making money. Trustworthiness in dealing, love of fair play, practical common sense, applied from day to day in business and in living, have made them, as sojourners or as citizens, a valuable asset.

Whatever elements in the character of our race contributed to this result, a field was given to them and a training-ground in bygone days and in foreign lands near home. It all enured to the coming time. From city to city the merchants went : they adjusted themselves and their little machinery of self-government, their courts, their settlements of disputes, their giving and taking, to one set of conditions in this place, to another in that. When the time came to play the human drama on a great scale far beyond the seas, the way to play it, on sound business lines, without overacting the parts, had been taught by the Merchant Adventurers of England.

CHAPTER IV

THE EASTLAND MERCHANTS

THE long continuity, which marked the life of the Merchant Adventurers of England, was wanting in the case of the Eastland Company. The charter, which Queen Elizabeth gave to the company in 1579, made no mention of previous royal grants, extended and renewed. Yet, like the Merchant Adventurers, the Eastland Merchants claimed, and could in some sort substantiate, an ancient ancestry.

Antiquity of the Baltic trade.

In a representation which the company made to Cromwell in January 1655–6, they asserted that they had discovered the trade to the Baltic seas 301 years earlier,[1] that is in 1354 or 1355, about the date when the Statute of the Staple was passed. In the Treaty of Utrecht with the Hanse cities in 1474, which included Dantzic and the Prussian trade, it was provided that the dues to be levied should not be higher than had existed a century or more before.[2] We are told that ships from the port of Hull traded to the Baltic in 1372, the northern and eastern ports of England being, as was natural, always specially concerned in this

---

[1] *Cal. S. P. Dom.*, 1655–6, 4 January, p. 97. (See below, p. 174.)

[2] See Rymer, under date 20 July 1474.

north-eastern trade;[1] and the pages of Hakluyt[2] give abundant evidence that in the fourteenth century, at any rate from the time of Edward III, dealings, or rather disputes, between English and Prussian merchants and seafarers were constant and manifold. Hakluyt gives an agreement concluded in 1388 between representatives of the King of England and of the 'Master-General of the land of Prussia', the head of the Teutonic Knights, which was confirmed by Richard II in 1390, and renounced again by the Master-General in 1398. The Prussian representatives spoke of wrongs done to their countrymen by the English in the reign of Edward III, and of a recent outrage in which the English had replied to Prussian complaints, 'Lo, in your own country of Prussia there are English merchants, and goods sufficient,'and had bidden them take in compensation two for one. A little later, in 1404, King Henry IV writes to the Master-General of 'the ancient friendship and love, which hath continued a long time between our realm and your territories and dominions', though the antiquity was probably exaggerated, as well as the love—after the manner of kings in the olden time. The Baltic towns which figure in these early negotiations are Dantzic and Elburg, later called Elbing;

Relations between England and Prussia in the latter part of the fourteenth and beginning of the fifteenth centuries.

[1] As an illustration, in the Act of 1566 incorporating anew the Russia Company, special reference is made to York, Newcastle, Hull, and Boston.

[2] See Hakluyt, vol. ii, pp. 12, &c.: the quotations given are on pp. 15 and 42.

these two towns were always most prominent in the record of the Eastland Merchants, Dantzic being chief among the easternmost cities of the Hanseatic League.

Henry IV and the Eastland.

Henry IV, while still only Henry of Bolingbroke, Earl of Derby, before he ousted his cousin King Richard II from the throne of England, had in the years 1390–2 gone crusading in the ranks of the Teutonic Knights. He therefore knew the Eastland with a personal knowledge, and after he became king, at the beginning of the fifteenth century, we find various agreements with the Master-General in 1405, 1407–8, 1409, and grants to the English merchants who traded into the Baltic; but the first grant of the kind which is recorded was made by Richard II on the 17th of January 1391, and no doubt followed upon the king's confirmation in the previous year of the agreement which had been concluded with the Prussian representatives. It was a grant or licence confirming the election of John Bebys, a citizen of London, as governor of the English merchants sojourning in Prussia, the regions of Lescone and the Sound, and the dominions of the Hanse, and giving the merchants authority to elect a governor annually.[1]

The charter of 1391.

In the year 1689 Nathaniel Tench, 'a very grave intelligent and worthy citizen and merchant',[2] who

---

[1] See Rymer under the date given.
[2] Strype's edition of Stow's *Survey*, vol. ii, Bk. V, pp. 262–3.

had been for many years governor of the Eastland
Company, wrote a 'very rational tract',[1] giving
an account and justification of the company. 'The
trade of this nation', the pamphlet says, 'was
formerly (as it were entirely) in the foreigners'
hands, viz. the members of the Hans towns, who
were incorporated into a society by the name of
the Merchants of the Dutch Hans. . . . About
the time of King Henry IV the English began to
trade themselves into the East parts', and the king,
'for the better encouragement of his own subjects,
did in the 5th year of his reign grant his first
charter to the merchants trading into the Eastland'.[2] This dates the Eastlanders from 1404. The
The grant of the 6th of June in that year speaks charters
of the merchants sojourning in the parts of Prussia, of 1404,
of Scone,[3] and in other parts of the Hanse; and

[1] See note 2 on previous page.

[2] The pamphlet is entitled *Reasons humbly offered by the Governor,
Assistants, and Fellowship of Eastland Merchants against the giving of
a general liberty to all persons whatsoever to export the English woollen
manufactures whither they please.* It is among the tracts on wool at
the British Museum, 712. g. 16. According to Cawston and Keane
(p. 61 note), the Eastland, or the East country, in old records
meant the region beyond the Vistula. Anderson (i. 420) speaks of
the East country as 'a name of old, and still given by mercantile
people, to the ports of the Baltic Sea, but more especially in Prussia
and Livonia'. See also Hakluyt (vol. i, p. 15), 'Wolstan's navigation
in the East Sea', where the East Sea is taken in the marginal note to
be 'within the Sound of Denmark', and Eastland is identified with
Lithuania.

[3] Sconia and Sconeland will be found referred to in Hakluyt (vol. ii,
pp. 42, 44, 46, 69), and was apparently important in connexion with
the herring fishery. Presumably it was Scania, now Skåne (German
Schonen) in the south of Sweden, which was Danish territory until

of 1408, there is a third charter, dated the 1st of March 1408, applying to the English merchants in Norway, Sweden, and Denmark.[1] This last charter was granted in the year after Henry IV gave the Merchant Adventurers their charter, to which it refers, and all these grants of 1391, 1404, 1407, and 1408 are on the same lines: they made provision for good government, and were not concerned with trade monopoly. The charter of 1404 was confirmed by King Henry VI on the 20th of June of 1428, 1428; but the Eastland Company, as known to history, did not come into existence until the year and of 1579, when, on the 7th of August, Queen Elizabeth incorporated 'The Governor, Assistants, and Fellowship of Merchants of Eastland'.[2]

the middle of the seventeenth century. Possibly Landskrone may have something to do with Lescone.

[1] As given in Rymer, the grant of 1391 applies to 'mercatores regni nostri Angliae in terra Pruciae, et in partibus de Lescone, Sounde, et in dominiis de Hansa commorantes'; the grant of 1404, to 'mercatores etc. in partibus Prussiae et de Scone ac in aliis partibus de Hansa commorantes'; the grant of 1408, to 'mercatores etc. in partibus Norwegiae, Sweciae et Daciae commorantes'. Henry VI's charter of 1428 purports to recite and confirm the grant of 1404, but recites it as 'in partibus Pruciae, Daciae, Norweiae, Hansae et Swechiae commorantes', thus combining the charters of 1404 and 1408. Hakluyt (ii, pp. 106–10), professing to give the 1404 charter, gives in the body of the charter the 1428 version; but gives in the heading a slightly different version again, 'Carta Henrici Quarti anno quinto regni sui concessa mercatoribus Angliae in partibus Prussiae, Daciae, Norwegiae, Swethiae, et Germaniae, de gubernatore inter ipsos ibidem constituendo'.

[2] A long extract from this charter is printed in the Appendix to *The Acts and Ordinances of the Eastland Company*, by Miss Maud Sellers, Royal Historical Society, 1906, pp. 142–51. Miss Sellers's book

Eastland, the Eastlands, the East countries, denoted the towns and regions bordering on the Baltic, reached by trading vessels through the Sound, the generic name being borne by Esthland or Esthonia. There is a charter given by Charles I to the City of London in October 1638, in which the Eastland Company is referred to as 'the governors and assistants of the English merchants trafficking in the Baltic Sea'. The complaint against the London Merchant Adventurers, embodied in the preamble of the Act of 1496, enumerated Danske (Dantzic) and Eastland among the 'divers coasts and parts beyond the sea', to which English merchants freely plied their trade. When the Eastland Company came into being, political conditions in the Baltic were widely different from those of the present day. Russia was not then a Baltic power, and Prussia was in infancy. Denmark, Sweden, Poland and Lithuania, the Hanse cities, were leading on the shores or in the islands of these Eastern seas. Leiffland, Livland, or Livonia: Pommern, Pommerland, or Pomerania: stood for more than, as now, the names of Russian or German provinces. Meanwhile, in England, the Muscovy or Russia Company had received a charter from Philip and Mary in 1555, and had been incorporated by Act of Parliament [1] in Queen Elizabeth's

Conditions under which the charter of 1579 was granted.

is invaluable, as the only book which gives full and accurate information on the subject of the Eastland Company; the account given in the text is mainly derived from it.

[1] 8 Eliz., cap. 17 (on Roll in Chancery). An Act for the corporation

reign, in 1566. In 1564 the Merchant Adventurers
of England had received a new charter; and in
1578 Queen Elizabeth had finally cancelled the
special privileges which the Hanse merchants had
almost from time immemorial enjoyed in England.
All these conditions were reflected in the terms of
the Eastland charter of 1579; it was designed
to strengthen English trading enterprise against
the foreigners, by combining the English merchants
concerned, who had received separate charters in
Henry IV's reign, while safeguarding the rights
of existing combinations.

The scope of the Eastland charter.

The preamble shows that it was a voluntary
union or federation of all the English merchants,
who dealt with the lands and peoples within the
Sound, other than the Muscovy merchants. All
these merchants, so the charter alleged, desired
to form 'one fellowship and commonalty and to
be one body incorporate and politic in deed and
in name', as well for the better government of
themselves as for the honour of England and her
queen. There were the merchants 'trading the East
parts commonly called the Dantzick merchants
or merchants trading in or through the Sound';
there were the merchants trading through the
Sound to Norway, Sweden, Poland, to 'Letto and
Leifland under the dominions of the King of
Powle Prussen', to Pomerland eastward from the

of Merchant Adventurers for the discovery of new trades. The Act will
be found in Hakluyt, vol. iii, pp. 83-91.

Oder, to specified Baltic ports, to Copenhagen and
Elsinore in Denmark; there were the traders to
various [islands within the Sound, among which
Finland was included, for, in spite of many years
of trading, the geography of the Baltic lands was
indifferently known in England at this date. From
Narva on the Gulf of Finland, with the territories
belonging to it, the Eastland Company was excluded; for, though not then belonging to Russia,
those territories had been placed within the sphere
of the Russia Company, in order—so it was said
—to obviate the mischief caused by Interlopers,
'a number of straggling merchants and unskilful
traders,'[1] who had put in an appearance at Narva

[1] See the pamphlet of 1689, *Reasons humbly offered, &c. (ut sup.)*,
pp. 5–6. Parker, in *A Discourse concerning Freedom of Trade (ut sup.)*,
p. 13, writes: 'The English had at the Narre in Leifland a good
trade, and good sales for our native commodities for a while, but about
1565 divers straggling merchants resorted thither out of England
and so brought themselves, and their wares, into great contempt.'
Hence, he says, the Lords of the Council at the next Parliament were
obliged to include 'the Narre' within the Muscovy Company's charter.
Hakluyt gives 'A letter of M. Henrie Lane', in which it is said 'the
first traffic to the Narve in Livonia' was in 1560 (iii, p. 335). He also
tells us that in 1567 Anthony Jenkinson secured from the Emperor of
Russia privileges for English merchants to trade at Narva, which
were renewed in 1569 (iii. 93–5, 109, 117). In 1576 it was said that
'the traffic at that place standeth upon the agreement and liking of
the Emperor of Russia, with the King of Sweden' (iii. 207). Narva
was a border town and territory, which was constantly passed from
one hand to another. Apparently, at the time of the Eastland Company's charter, it was under Sweden, though belonging in right to
Russia. Thus the Committee of Council for Trade and Navigation in
June 1656 recommended that the town and territories of Narva,
which were not in the former charter (the Eastland charter of 1579),
as then belonging to Russia, and therefore granted to the Muscovy
Company, should be now granted to the Eastland Company, as

in the previous year, caused disturbances and spoiled the trade. The interests of the Merchant Adventurers were safeguarded, as has been told,[1] by constituting all Denmark, with the exception of Copenhagen and Elsinore, together with the lands between the Elbe and the Oder, neutral ground open to both companies. The Eastlanders were to be allowed to use the Elbe for the transport of their goods, but they were not to break bulk or conduct any sales along that river or at Hamburg.

Qualification for membership.

The rules laid down for membership are most difficult to understand : there are so many qualifications and exceptions. All the members of the company were to be British subjects and, as in the case of the Merchant Adventurers, merchants in the true sense, 'mere merchants', not retailers nor handicraftsmen. Apparently the original members were to consist of such merchants as had traded through the Sound before the 1st of January 1568. As to new members, the general rule was to be that no merchants were to be admitted to the fellowship who were 'free of any other company or society trading merchandise beyond the seas'. All merchants who did not belong to other companies were to be admitted on application, if they had

belonging to Sweden (*Cal. S. P. Dom.*, 1655-6, p. 346. See below, pp. 174-5). For the changes in the Baltic provinces, see Freeman's *Historical Geography of Europe*. According to Freeman's maps Narva would seem to have been in Esthland ; but, as seen above, Parker placed it in Leifland or Livonia, and so did the letter from Henry Lane.

[1] See above, p. 118, and note.

traded to the Eastland through the Sound in any
one year since the 1st of January 1568 and applied
within one year from the date of the charter, on
payment of £6 13s. 4d., otherwise on payment of
£20; and in the case of merchants resident in
Bristol, Exeter, Barnstaple, Lyme, Dartmouth,
Plymouth, Bridgewater, Seaton, and Totnes, these
provisions were to apply, whether they belonged
to another company or not. Evidently those who
inspired the charter wished to conciliate the clothmaking interest of the West Country and the
Western ports, at a later date so prolific of complaints against London and against the Merchant Special
Adventurers. The Merchant Adventurers, and provision
for Mer-
merchant traders to Spain and Portugal, received chant
Adven-
preferential treatment—those at least among them turers.
who had traded through the Sound since 1568:
they were to be admitted, if they applied within
one year from the date of the charter, on payment
of £10. These same merchants, if not thus qualified,
were to be admitted on payment of 40 marks, a
larger sum than the ordinary fee for merchants
not being members of any other company trading
beyond the sea. The general prohibition against
members of other companies was rendered practically nugatory, partly by the exceptions already
specified, partly by further provisions to the effect
that a member of another company trading to
foreign parts might become an Eastlander, either
by paying to the Eastland fellowship the same

redemption or admission fee as his own company
exacted from new members, or by giving up his
own company in exchange for the Eastland fellowship, or by reciprocity if he procured free admission
of an Eastlander into his own company as against
his own admission into the Eastland Company, the
second and third alternatives being provisions for
admission without any entrance fee.   It must in
charity be supposed that the original draft of the
charter was not so complicated and inept as its
final form ; that it started with a clear exclusion
of members of other companies, unless, perhaps,
they were Merchant Adventurers ; that one interest
and another procured exceptions, and that the
eventual result was—perhaps as the best solution
under the circumstances—hardly intelligible.[1]

Organiza-   The courts of the company might be held ' as
tion and
privileges   well within some convenient place within our city
of the
company.   of London or elsewhere within our dominions as
also within the said realms and dominions of the
East parts aforesaid ', and the government was
vested in a governor and twenty-four assistants,
who were empowered to make laws for and levy
dues upon, not only members of the fellowship,
but also all British subjects trading to the same
parts, provided that the laws were not repugnant
to the laws of England, and did not conflict with
treaty rights and obligations.   To the company

---

[1] These provisions will be found on pp. 146-9 of Miss Sellers's book,
and her comments on pp. xv–xvi of the Preface.

thus constituted and organized was granted the monopoly of the Eastland trade.

Cloth, it need hardly be said, was the main English export to the Baltic, though skins and other articles were exported too. ' Neither is here to be omitted that company, which is called the Eastland Company, whose principal trading also consists in the same commodity of woollen cloths, by which they do furnish all those Eastern countries about the Baltic Sea.' This was written as late as 1675, and the writer breaks into doggerel :

The East-
land
trade.

' And all the Eastlands o'er such is the trade
  For Woollen clothes, in England which are
    made.' [1]

Imports play a more prominent part in the records of the Eastland Company than in those of the Merchant Adventurers. Everything that is told of the Adventurers' trade is concerned with the export of cloth : all the complaints brought against them deal with the export traffic only. But in the Baltic the Eastlanders were trading with lands of raw products rather than with manufacturing centres, and what they brought into England was at least as important as what they took out. William Cholmeley, in his pamphlet of 1553,[2] writes of ' masts, waynescote, hemp, pitch, tar, ashes, wax,

---

[1] *An Essay to the restoring of our Decayed Trade, &c.*, by Joseph Trevers, 1675, pp. 9, 58.

[2] *The Request and Suite of a True-hearted Englishman*, p. 10. See above, pp. 95–7.

flax, copper, iron, and corn which cometh so
plenteously out of Poland'. Timber, tallow, and
cordage were brought back in the English ships,
and Eastland corn fed the markets both of England
and of the Low Countries.[1]

The mart
at Elbing.
The company prospered for a while, but only for
a short while. We are told that in the reigns of
Queen Elizabeth, James I, and Charles I it was
known as the Royal Company.[2] Elbing, on a
small river running into the gulf of Dantzic, east
of the delta of the Vistula, was chosen to be the
head-quarters and distributing centre in the Baltic,
and the Eastlanders were known as the merchants
of Elbing.[3] As Stade gained an abnormal and
transitory prosperity by becoming for a few years
the home of the Merchant Adventurers, so, in
Camden's words, Elbing owed 'a great part of its
beauty and splendour, and the vast confluence of
people thither, purely to the trade and intercourse
of the English'.[4] Apparently it was intended to

[1] See, e.g., for the importance of the Eastland corn trade in
Henry VIII's reign, *State Papers King Henry VIII*, vol. xi, 1852,
pp. 75, 80, 92. See above, p. 83.

[2] 'Heretofore the East Country company, above all others, was the
most flourishing; and by Queen Elizabeth, King James, and King
Charles I, termed the Royal Company, for it supplied Muscovy,
Sweden, Denmark, Poland, and Lifeland with our woollen manufactures,' &c. *England's Improvements*, Treatise III, by Roger Coke,
1675, pp. 32-3.

[3] 'The company of merchants trading to the East country, called
commonly in Queen Elizabeth's time the merchants of Elbing,
because there they first seated themselves.' Strype, *ut sup.*, vol. ii,
Bk. V, p. 262.

[4] Camden's *History of Queen Elizabeth* in *A Complete History of*

be the sole mart in the Eastlands for the importation of English wares; but the river was small,
a more commodious centre was desired, and in
1622 an Order in Council was passed authorizing
the removal from Elbing to Dantzic or elsewhere
in the Baltic. From this date onward there does
not seem to have been any one centre to the exclusion of others. Though Dantzic was probably
the most important mart, Königsberg, Riga, Revel,
and other places were important too.

But already, in King James I's reign, the Eastlanders showed signs of distress. On the 26th of
June 1620 they petitioned the king that the
importation into England of the goods in which
they dealt might be prohibited in any but English
ships, which meant excluding all ships but their
own. They averred that the Hollanders had engrossed the trade by the cheapness of their freights,
and that the sale of English cloth in the Eastland
had fallen in value from £200,000 to £70,000 or
£80,000 per annum.[1] Their representations carried The Pro-
weight, and on the 21st of July 1622 the king clamation
issued a Proclamation prohibiting 'the bringing in of 21 July
of any commodities traded by the Eastland mer- 1622,
chants into this kingdom, as well by subjects as
strangers, not free of that company', and enforcing

England, 1706 ed., vol. ii, p. 601. In this passage Camden tells us
that George Carew, on a political mission to the Baltic, visited Elbing
in 1598. ' Here he had the good luck to compromise matters in some
measure between the citizens of that place and the English factory.'
[1] See *Cal. S. P. Dom.*, 1619–23, p. 157, 26 June 1620.

the old Navigation Acts, as being ' divers good and
politic laws, made against the shipping of merchandises in strangers bottoms '. One notable exception, however, was made. It was provided 'that
the importation of corn and grain be left free and
without restraint '. So necessary to England were
food supplies from overseas, even in the early years
of the seventeenth century, and so important was
the corn trade of the Baltic.[1] This Proclamation
and of dealt with imports only. In the following reign,
7 March however, on the 7th of March 1629, it was renewed
1629. and enlarged so as to include exports also.[1] Again
the Navigation Acts were enforced, and again the
free import of corn was safeguarded.

King James, who came to the company's aid with
his Proclamation of 1622, had been indirectly in
great measure the cause of its difficulties. The
Eastlanders traded farther afield than the Merchant Adventurers, and ran correspondingly greater
risks. Four months was given as the average time
for a trading voyage to the Baltic.[2] They traded
through the Sound, and for the security of their
vessels and cargoes they depended largely upon
The dyed the goodwill of Denmark. But what troubled them
cloth con- most was Dutch competition. This had either been
troversy
and Dutch called into being, or at any rate greatly stimulated,
competi-
tion.

[1] These Proclamations are printed in the Appendices to Miss Sellers's
book, pp. 151-3, and 153-5.
[2] See *England's Improvements* (*ut sup.*), Treatise IV, ' How the
Navigation of England may be increased,' &c., p. 98.

by the king's ill-advised and ill-fated attempt,
already noticed,[1] to substitute a new company for
the Merchant Adventurers. In the charter which
he gave to his new company he carefully safeguarded the rights of 'the merchants commonly
called the merchants of Eastland'. Yet none
suffered more from the policy which the charter
embodied than these selfsame Eastland merchants.
Free Trade and Protection are no new terms. The
controversy between Free Traders and Protectionists
has raged through all the centuries and all the
nations. The partisans have taken one name and
another, and have put forward pleas deduced from
the particular time and place and trade. The
Staplers had to face a growing cry that English
wool should be kept in England, to foster English
instead of foreign manufactures. The Merchant
Adventurers, in turn, had to face a similar contention that all the processes connected with the cloth
trade should be perfected in England, before the
cloth was shipped abroad, so as to employ English
and not alien handicraftsmen. Both before King
James's time and afterwards the question as to
how far the export of English cloth should be confined to dyed and dressed cloth was argued back
and fore ; and the preference which it was desired
to give to dyed cloth can be traced in the Eastland charter, in which no limit was placed upon
the amount of coloured and dressed cloth to be

[1] See above, pp. 97–100.

exported, whereas the export of white dressed cloths was limited to 200 per annum.[1] There were strenuous upholders of the policy of insisting upon the export of dyed cloth, and they were no lovers of the Merchant Adventurers who were in the other camp. 'All the companies of the land transport cloths dressed and dyed to the good of the kingdom (except the Merchant Adventurers), whereby the Easterland and Turkey merchants with other companies do increase customs by bringing in and spending dyeing stuffs and setting people on work by dressing and dyeing afore they transport them.'[2] This was the view of a pamphleteer in 1650. But, as has been seen, King James's attempt to prohibit the export of undyed and undressed cloth had only the effect of bringing the Dutch into competition with English cloth makers and cloth exporters ; and, even as Flemish immigrants into England taught the English the making of cloths, so English immigrants into the Netherlands, Nonconformist families from East Anglia, men and women such as freighted the *Mayflower* for North America, taught the Dutchmen in turn.

Decline of the company.

Dutch competition, coupled with the Civil Wars in England, coupled too with the fact that the Eastland peoples themselves, Silesians and Polanders,

[1] The restriction, judging from the terms of the charter, was also imposed in the interests of the Merchant Adventurers, who were not so restricted.

[2] From *A clear and evident way for enriching the nations of England and Ireland*, 1650, p. 13.

took to making their own cloths, brought a speedy
decline to the prosperity of the Eastland Company.
' We send into the East kingdoms yearly but 100
ships', says the writer of 1650 who has been quoted
above, ' and our trade chiefly dependeth upon three
towns, Elbing, Kingsborough, and Dantzick. . . .
The Low Countries send into the East kingdoms
yearly about 3000 ships, trading into every city
and port town.' [1] A later account, published in or
about 1670, states that the English Eastland trade
had fallen by half, the Dutch had increased ten-
fold [2]; and yet another of five years later is to the
effect, ' Whereas before the year 1640 the Eastland
Company vended yearly 20000 broad clothes, they
now do not 4000 ; of 60000 kerseys, now not 5000 ;
of 40000 Doubles, now not 2000.' [3] According to
this last authority, Roger Coke, Suffolk and Essex,
especially the district round Ipswich, to which in
the reign of King James I the Eastland trade
had brought prosperity, at the time when he

[1] *A clear and evident way, &c. (ut sup.)*, p. 8.

[2] Sir Josiah Child's statement, which was written, but not published,
in 1665, quoted by Macpherson, ii. 544.

[3] *England's Improvements*, Treatise III, by Roger Coke (*ut sup.*),
p. 33. See also Treatise II, *Reasons of the Increase of the Dutch
Trade*, by the same, 1671, in which he writes (p. 111): ' The Dutch,
finding themselves hereby deprived of the benefit of dyeing and
dressing our white clothes, fell into the way of making cloth, and set
up looms and fulling mills at great charges ; and procured workmen
from England, Flanders, and other places ; whereby in a few years
they so improved these manufactures at home, that they made most
of the fine cloth used in these parts of Europe, besides great quanti
ties of coarse cloth, and innumerable pieces of stuffs of all sorts.'

wrote, 1675, participated in its decay. Seeing
that the latter part of the seventeenth century
was marked by three wars between Great Britain
and the Netherlands, English vessels trading
through the Sound must have suffered much at the
hands of De Ruyter's countrymen. Pepys tells us
in August 1665 of 'the good news that all our
ships, which were in such danger that nobody
would ensure upon them, from the Eastland, were
all safe arrived', which he considered a great
piece of good luck in view of the loss of the
Hamburg fleet in the previous May; and in October
of the same year he writes that the Dutch fleet
was reported at the Texel 'in expectation of our
Eastland ships coming home with masts and
hemp, and our loaden Hambrough ships going to
Hambrough'.[1]

The latter days of the company.   There is little more to be told. From about
1656–60 the company was in a state of suspended
animation. In January 1656 we find them petitioning Cromwell for confirmation of their privileges
and for further regulation of the Baltic trade, in
order to put an end to 'a licentious and confused
kind of commerce'.[2] In June of that year the
Council of State was favourable to renewing their
charter, and made the suggestion that the Protector
should use his personal influence to transfer Narva
to them from the Russia Company, as the East-

[1] *Pepys's Diary* (*ut sup.* See above, p. 109), vol. v (1895), pp. 57, 100.
[2] *Cal. S. P. Dom.*, 1655-6, pp. 97 (see above, p. 156) and 346.

landers had long traded to Narva by connivance.[1]
In 1661 Charles II renewed the charter,[2] but not
the failing fortunes; and by an Act passed in
1672 his parliament dealt a crushing blow to the
unfortunate company. The Act provided that, from
the 1st of May 1673, the trade with Sweden,
Denmark, and Norway should be thrown open to
all, whether British subjects or aliens, and that
all British subjects should be admitted to the
fellowship of Merchants of Eastland on payment
of a sum of forty shillings.[3] Thus Scandinavia was
eliminated altogether from the company's monopoly,
and permission to trade with the regions where
the charter still held good could be obtained for
a nominal sum. In spite of this blow, however,
the company still retained some life. The pam-
phlets of 1675, which have been quoted, show
that if, according to one account, it was then in
a state of decay, according to another it still busily
supplied the Baltic lands with English cloth.[4] Its

The Act of 1672.

[1] See note 2 on previous page.

[2] 20 February 1661. 1661 is the date assigned by the British Museum
to the undated pamphlet, *Reasons offered by the Merchants Adventurers
of England and Eastland Merchants residing at Hull for the preservation
of their societies and regulations as being reasonable just and necessary
to the liberal and profitable vent of our native manufactures in the
foreign parts limited to them by their charters* (B. M. 816 m. $\frac{11}{100}$).

[3] 25 Charles II, cap. 7, secs. 5, 6. The Act is entitled, 'An act for
the encouragement of the Greenland and Eastland Trades, and for the
better securing the Plantation Trade'.

[4] Contrast the quotation given from Roger Coke's *England's
Improvements*, on p. 173, with that from Joseph Trevers's *An Essay to
the Restoring of our Decayed Trade*, on p. 167.

charter is safeguarded in an Act of 1688, the first year of William and Mary;[1] and we have seen that in the following year, 1689, its governor powerfully pleaded its cause.[2] Strype tells us that the courts were held at the Founders Hall in Lothbury; that the governor, deputy governor, and twenty-four assistants were annually chosen on the first Wednesday after Michaelmas Day, and he enumerates the articles exported and imported, from which it must be inferred that the members of the fellowship still did some business at the time when he published his edition of Stow, the year 1720.[3] But in the course of the eighteenth century the Eastland Company became no more than a name; and when Macpherson published his *Annals of Commerce* in 1805, he recorded that 'they do not now exist commercially, or otherwise, but in name only, which it seems they still keep up, by continuing to elect their annual officers; and having (like the Merchants of the Staple, another company in similar circumstances) a little stock in our public funds, the interest thereof defrays the expenses of their annual meetings'.[4] Like the Staplers, the Eastlanders faded away, but when their existence finally came to an end is not known.

[1] 1 Will. and M., cap. 32, sec. 13. 'An act for the better preventing the exportation of wool and encouraging the woollen manufactures of this kingdom.'

[2] *Reasons humbly offered, &c. (ut sup.),* pp. 158-9.

[3] Bk. V, p. 262. [4] Vol. ii, p. 165.

Many of the Eastlanders, probably the large majority, were Merchant Adventurers also. The terms of the Eastland charter imply that this was contemplated; and we read of joint meetings of the members of the two fellowships, especially when the local patriotism of a provincial city, in which both Eastlanders and Merchant Adventurers were represented, was aroused against London. The two companies too, though wholly distinct from one another, had various features in common; and no doubt, when the Eastland charter was drafted, those who inspired it had in view the Merchant Adventurers' charter of 1564. The governing body in either case consisted of a governor and twenty-four assistants. In either case the main strength of the fellowship was in London, and outside London the members of either fellowship were to be found in much the same cities, principally in the north and east of England. There was the same standing feud between the provincial centres and London, and in the year 1616 the Eastland Merchants of the coast towns, the ' Coast-men ' as they were termed—York, Ipswich, Newcastle, and Hull being specially mentioned—procured an important decision from the King's Council to the effect that by-laws and constitutions for the fellow-ship were, except in case of emergency, to be passed only once a year at a Court in London at which the coast towns were to be represented, though without the right of voting; and the ordinances or by-laws were to be approved by the Lord Chancellor, the Lord Treasurer, and two Chief Justices.

But, if there were points of similarity between the companies, there were also fundamental differences. Whatever influence London enjoyed in the counsels of the Merchant Adventurers—and its influence was great—it has been seen that the governing body was resident beyond the sea. The Eastland Company, on the contrary, was governed avowedly and exclusively from London, with no diversities of freedom, no graded privileges among the members. There were local bodies of Eastlanders, 'residences' as they were termed, in other English towns, and deputy governors were appointed to them; but the appointments were made from London, though local nominees were in the ordinary course appointed. The right of having a Court of Assistants was denied to the provincial residences, the refusal leading to a protracted controversy between York and London. The deputy governors beyond the seas had the right of choosing twelve assistants, but they and their assistants were entirely under London control. The oath which the members of the fellowship took bound them to have respect to 'the mind and agreement of the governor, or his deputy, and assistants resident in London'.[1] London was the fount of all authority, the centre of all control.

The Eastland Company was governed from London,

---

[1] See Dendy (*ut sup.*), ii. 181.

Nor had the general body of the fellowship, inside London or outside, at any rate in actual practice, the same power as was possessed by the general body of the Merchant Adventurers. The Eastlanders outside London had no vote at the general meetings, and the general meetings seem to have been composed mainly of the governing body. 'The power of ruling the whole company, of making by-laws, and appointing officers is by the charter vested in the Court of Assistants only, and if all the generality of the company were present, they could have no voice in any question.' [1] This was the pronouncement of the London autocrats to the recalcitrant men of York. They might have added that the Court of Assistants in effect elected themselves, for this seems to have been the case. No such despotic régime existed among the Merchant Adventurers, and this was due to the fact that the head-quarters were not in London.

and the general body of the fellowship had no power.

The Eastlanders were British merchants and were therefore required to be British subjects, but the stringent conditions against marrying foreign wives and holding foreign property, by which the Adventurers were bound, seem to have been wanting in the other case. The Eastland Fellowship, in short, had little of the national character which gave width and greatness to the Merchant Adventurers ; and, as compared with the long unbroken history of the

The Eastlanders not a national company in the sense of the Merchant Adventurers.

[1] Letter from London to York, 20 February 1691. Sellers (*ut sup.*), p. 136.

Adventurers, few and for the most part evil were the days of the Eastlanders' working life. Yet they must be given a place in any account of the beginnings of English enterprise beyond the seas, seeing that they or their forbears, in trading to the Baltic, carried the wares and the name of England far afield, and that the first clear and definite mention of a governor being elected by English citizens in foreign parts, and of his election being confirmed by an English king, was when the Eastlander John Bebys was approved by Richard II as governor of the English merchants sojourning in Prussia.

CHAPTER V

CONCLUSION

SUCH were the beginnings of English overseas
enterprise; and out of it came in fullness of time
the British Empire. We are told, in our histories,
of the wars which the English waged, for a hundred
years more or less, to keep their hold on France.
Creçy, Poitiers, Agincourt, stand out in our annals
for the fame which they brought to the fighting
men of England. But they were no more than
glorious incidents in a complete though most
salutary failure, the inevitable failure of an island
people to work out a destiny on continental lines.
We are not told how meanwhile the future of Great
Britain was beginning to be shaped in wholly
different fashion; how the merchants were teaching,
better than they knew, that it was to be a future
of penetration by trade and settlement not by conquest, that it was to be the work of English citizens
not of English kings, not the result of definitive
State policy, not of strong action by determined
rulers and resolute governments, but a slow process
of compromise between war and peace, between
private initiative and State control, such a com-

promise as commended itself day by day to the
practical instincts of a liberty-loving island race.

Because the English lived on an island, therefore
they failed when they attempted aggrandizement
as though they were on a continent, as though
the Straits of Dover had no existence. But because
they lived on an island, when they recognized that
they must move forward in other directions and
on other lines than continental peoples, the island
home enabled them to do so with a security denied
to all the other peoples of the world. Hence has
come the wonderful continuity of English history,
the evolution, the growth, the perpetual widening
out. Continuity of geography does not necessarily
make for continuity of history: rather it makes
against it. The histories of continental nations
have rarely run the course prescribed by nature.
They have been hurried or hindered, forced or
stunted, turned out of the straight road by conflict
with or contagion from adjacent rival peoples.
Alone among the older nations of the world,
England has grown in unbroken continuity, on
its own natural lines in its own human way.
Alone in all the centuries it has grown from an
island into an Empire, even as the acorn becomes
the oak, and this island Empire, the only island
Empire that the world has so far seen, is unique in
kind, an Empire in name, in fact a greater England.
This central truth of continuous growth should
be the rock on which our histories are built. It

should be as the stone thrown into the water, the centre of ever-widening circles. The past should be written and read as the prelude to the Empire, and the first pioneers of the Empire will be found not among the conquering kings of the Middle Ages but in the Merchant Adventurers of England.

APPENDIX

CHARTER GRANTED BY HENRY IV TO THE ENGLISH MERCHANTS IN HOLLAND, ZEELAND, BRABANT, AND FLANDERS, FEBRUARY 5TH, 1406/7.

Translated from Rymer's *Foedera*, viii. 464.

On behalf of the merchants of Holland.

HENRY by the grace of God King of England and France and Lord of Ireland, to all to whom these present letters shall come, greeting.

Know ye that,

Whereas, according as we are informed, through want of good and discreet rule and government, sundry damages, strifes, oppressions and wrongs oftentimes heretofore have been moved and committed among the merchants of our kingdom of England, and of other of our dominions, remaining and sojourning in the parts of Holland, Zeland, Brabant and Flanders, and in whatsoever other parts beyond the seas being in amity with us, and greater hereafter (which God forbid) are feared to be like to fall out, unless we speedily put to our helping hands for the procuring of better government to be maintained among the said merchants,

We,

Heartily desiring to prevent the perils and dangers which are like to fall out in this case, and that the said merchants and others which shall travel out of our said realm and dominions into the parts aforesaid may justly and faithfully be ruled and entreated,

Do will and grant, by the tenor of these presents, to the said merchants, that they may freely and lawfully assemble and meet together, as often and whensoever they please, in some convenient and fitting place, where they shall think good, and that they may choose and elect among themselves certain sufficient and fit persons for their governors in those parts at their good liking ;

And furthermore we give and grant to the said Governors which are in such sort to be chosen by the aforesaid merchants, as much as in us lieth, special power and authority to rule and govern all and singular the merchants our subjects remaining in those parts and which hereafter shall come and repair to those parts, either by themselves or by their sufficient deputies, and to do unto them and every one of them in their causes and quarrels whatsoever, which are sprung up or shall hereafter spring up among them in the parts aforesaid, full and speedy justice,

And to reform, seek to amend, redress, appease and pacify all manner of questions, contentions, discords, and debates moved or to be moved between the merchants our subjects and the merchants of the parts aforesaid,

And to redress, repair, restore and amend all transgressions, damages, misprisions, outrages, violences and injuries done or to be done by the aforesaid merchants our subjects against the merchants of the parts aforesaid,

And to require, demand and receive the like

restitutions, reparations, restorations and amends of the merchants of the parts aforesaid or of their deputies,

And, by the common consent of the aforesaid merchants our subjects, to make and establish statutes, ordinances and customs as shall seem expedient in that behalf for the better government of the state of the said merchants our subjects,

And to punish reasonably according to the quantity of their offence in that behalf all and singular the merchants our subjects which shall withstand, resist or disobey the aforesaid governors so to be chosen, or their deputies, or any of them, or any of the aforesaid statutes, ordinances and customs,

Moreover we do ratify, confirm and approve, and as ratified, confirmed and approved we command firmly and inviolably then to be observed all just and reasonable statutes, ordinances and customs which shall be made and established by the said governors, so to be chosen, in the form aforesaid,

And also all just and reasonable ordinances made and established by the aforesaid merchants our subjects, with the common consent of the said merchants for this their government in the parts aforesaid, according to the privileges and authorities granted unto them by the Lords or Governors of the parts aforesaid, together or singly,

Or which shall be made and established by the aforesaid governors, now, as is mentioned, to be chosen according to the aforesaid privileges heretofore granted, or other privileges hereafter to be granted, to the said merchants our subjects by the aforesaid Lords or Governors, together or singly ;

And furthermore, by the tenor of these presents, we straitly command all and singular the aforesaid merchants our subjects, that they attend, advise, obey and assist, as it becometh them, the said governors so to be chosen, and their deputies, in all and singular the premisses and other reasonable things, which any way may concern in this behalf their rule and government.

Given in our Palace at Westminster under the testimony of our great Seal, the fifth day of February, in the year of the Lord one thousand four hundred and six, and in the eighth of our reign.

INDEX

Alderton (Northallerton), 41 *n.*
Alfred, King, 10.
Alien merchants, 33, 34, 34 *n.*, 36, 42 *n.*, 47, 70, 77, 115, 175 ; the Hansards, 89–91.
Almayne, merchants of, 89.
Alva, Duke of, 85.
American Historical Review, see Lingelbach, Dr.
Anderson, *An Historical and Geographical deduction of the Origin of Commerce from the earliest accounts to the present time* (1764), 15 *n.*, 16 *n.*, 23, 23 *n.*, 31 *n.*, 32 *n.*, 41 *n.*, 42 *n.*, 43, 43 *n.*, 44 *n.*, 55 *n.*, 61 *n.*, 127 *n.*, 138 *n.*, 159 *n.*
Anglo-Saxon kings, trade under, 10.
Antwerp—
Company of Staple at, 27 *n.*, 28.
Dyer from, in London, 96.
'English house' in, 83–4, 84 *n.*
English merchants arrested at, 85.
Entrepôt for English wool, 25, 26, 27 *n.*, 57.
First staple market perhaps held at, 24, 25 *n.*
Late packhouse of Europe, 88, 88 *n.*
Merchant Adventurers at, 57, 57 *n.*, 59, 64–6, 66 *n.*, 67, 68, 68 *n.*, 70, 74 *n.*, 85, 86, 123, 153 ; prohibition of Merchant Adventurers at, 86, 86 *n.*
Papist English merchants at, 109.
Sir Thomas Gresham at, 75–6.
State of the market at, in 1533, 75.
Apprentices, 120, 121.
Arbitrators of the staple, 34.

'Arragon', merchants of, 42.
Artois, 26, 28.
Ashes, 167.
Ashley, Professor, *An Introduction to English Economic History and Theory*, 25 *n.*
Assessors of the staple, 34, 34 *n.*
Auerstadt, 117.

Bacon, Francis, on English chartered companies, 147.
History of the Reign of King Henry VII (Ellis and Spedding), 67, 67 *n.*, 68, 68 *n.*
Letters and Life of Francis Bacon (Spedding), 98, 99, 100, and *notes.*
Bakers, 15 *n.*
Baltic Sea, 161, &c.
Baltic trade, antiquity of, 156–7.
Barnstaple, 165.
Bays, 112 *n.*
Bebys, John, 158, 180.
Becket, *see* St. Thomas Becket.
Bergen op Zoom, 49, 65, 65 *n.*
Berkshire, 50 *n.*
Berwick-on-Tweed, 41 *n.*, 54 *n.*
Blades, William, *Life and Typography of William Caxton*, 58 *n.*, 65 *n.*
Bland, Brown, and Tawney, *English Economic History, Select Documents*, 27 *n.*, 29 *n.*, 30 *n.*, 44 *n.*
Bolingbroke, Henry, Earl of Derby, afterwards Henry IV, q. **v.**
Books, 83.
Bordeaux, 126.
Boston (St. Botolph's *or* St. Botolph's town), 33, 38, 43, 136 *n.*, 157 *n.* ; *see also* Boystone.
Boystone (? Boston), 13 *n.*

Macpherson, &c. (*continued*)
  112 *n.*, 115 *n.*, 127 *n.*, 138 *n.*,
  176.
Magna Charta, 14, 14 *n.*, 16 *n.*
Maitland, *History of London*,
  22 *n.*, 44 *n.*, 57 *n.*
Malden, H. E., *The Cely Papers*;
  see under Cely Papers.
Malmesbury, *see* William of Mal-
  mesbury.
Malynes, Gerard, 52–3, 55, 61*n.*, 94.
  Center of the Circle of Commerce,
  13 *n.*, 45, 45 *n.*, 46, 46 *n.*, 49 *n.*,
  53 *n.*
  Maintenance of Free Trade, the,
  13 *n.*, 103, 103 *n.*
Margaret, Lady, Dowager Duchess
  of Burgundy, 67.
Marseilles, 9.
Mary, Queen, 40, 90, 91, 108 *n.*,
  129; *see also* Philip and
  Mary.
Masts, 167, 174.
Matilda of Flanders, 14.
Mayflower, the, 172.
Mayor of the staple, 30, 34, 35,
  35 *n.*, 37.
Mayor of staple town, 35.
Mayor of the town of Calais, 37.
Mecklenburg, 118 *n.*
Mediterranean, 42.
Melcombe, Dorset, 42 *n.*
Mercers' Company, 57, 58, 65,
  68–9, 74, 135.
  Hall, 58 *n.*
  Records, 58 *n.*
Merchant Adventurers—
  Antiquity and origin of, 22 *n.*,
  23, 57, 60.
  Antwerp and, *see* Antwerp.
  Brabant and, *see* Brabant.
  Bruges and, *see* Bruges.
  Calais and, *see* Calais.
  Caxton a governor, 65–6; *see
  also* Caxton.
  Charles I and, 105, 106, 113.
  Charles II and, 62*n.*, 63 *n.*, 107,
  108, 113.
  Charters, Proclamations, Licen-
  ces, &c., granted to or refer-
  ring to the Merchant Adven-
  turers (1248), 59, 62 *n.*;
  (1296), 22 *n.*, 57; (1358),

Merchant Adventurers (*continued*)
  59; (1359), 32 *n.*, 59 *n.*, 61 *n.*,
  62 *n.*; (140$\frac{6}{7}$, the 'first charter'), 61 *n.*, 62, 62 *n.*, 71, 102,
  141, 149–51, translation,
  184–7; (1413), 62 *n.*; (1420),
  62 *n.*; (1428), 62 *n.*; (1446),
  59, 63, 74; (1462), 23 *n.*, 62,
  62 *n.*, 63, 65; (1486), 66–7;
  (1496), 58, 58 *n.*, 63, 68–9, 71,
  75; 112, 120, 135, 140; (1505),
  45–7, 54 *n.*, 70–2, 73, 80, 121;
  (1506), 72, 73, 135; (1507), 73;
  (1520), 74, 74 *n.*; (155$\frac{8}{9}$), 77;
  (1563–74), 85 *n.*, 86 *n.*; (1564),
  73, 78–81, 87, 113, 118, 120,
  135, 140, 151, 162, 177;
  (1579, Eastland charter), 81,
  118, 165–6; (1582), 91 *n.*;
  (1586), 78, 81–3; (1587), 89 *n.*,
  91; (1596), 89 *n.*; (1597), 91;
  (1598), 91; (1604), 94; (1614),
  97; (1617), 99; (1618), 49–50,
  76, 100–3, 115; (1624), 104 *n.*,
  105 *n.*; (1634), 105, 113;
  (1643), 106, 106 *n.*; (1652),
  110, 111 *n.*, 112 *n.*; (1656),
  107, 112; (1661, the 'last
  charter'), 62 *n.*, 107; (1662),
  107–8; (1663), 108, 113.
  Cloth trade and, 12, 13, 78 *n.*,
  94, 103, 116.
  Cokayne's rival company, 98–
  100.
  Complaints, 111, 161.
  Cromwell and, *see* Cromwell.
  Decline, 107, 108, 116–17.
  Dispute about dyed and dressed
  goods, 97–8.
  Dort and, 93, 108, 111, 112, 112 *n.*
  Driven from Germany to the
  United Netherlands, 91–2.
  Early history, 15–19; 32 *n.* (in
  1359).
  Eastlanders and, 165–6, 167,
  177–80.
  Edward III and IV and, *see*
  Edward III and IV.
  Edward VI and, 75.
  Elizabeth and, *see* Elizabeth.
  Emden and, *see under* Emden.
  End of the company, 117.
  English homes, 124-5.

Wool (*continued*)
 Staple, 24, 28, 33, 37 *n.*, 43 ff., 51 ; *see also* Cloth.
Woolfels, 12, 29, 33, 37 *n.*, 50, 54, 54 *n.*
Woollen cloths, 23, 54 *n.*, 167–8.
Woollen manufacture, 12, 14, 57, 101, 108, 111, 112.
Worcester, 50 *n.*
Worcestershire, 99.
Wright, Thomas, *Political Poems and Songs from Edward III to Richard III*, 95 *n.*

Yarmouth, 38 ; *see also* Great Yarmouth.
York, 30 *n.*, 33, 38, 43, 119, 122, 124, 130, 132, 138.
 Eastlanders and, 177.
 Russia Company and, 157 *n.*
Yorkshire, 50 *n.*
Young, Thomas, 93, 94.

Zeeland, 39, 49, 61 *n.*, 63, 66, 69, 73, 77, 78, 92, 96, 118, 121, 125.
 Printer to States of, 59 *n.*, 92.

PRINTED IN ENGLAND
AT THE OXFORD UNIVERSITY PRESS